The London Rambler and Footpath Guide to the surrounding districts. Reprinted (with additions) by permission from the "Echo.'.

Howard Evans

The London Rambler and Footpath Guide to the surrounding districts ... Reprinted (with additions) by permission from the "Echo.'.
Evans, Howard
British Library, Historical Print Editions
British Library
1884
89 p. ; 8°.
10350.bbb.28.

The BiblioLife Network

This project was made possible in part by the BiblioLife Network (BLN), a project aimed at addressing some of the huge challenges facing book preservationists around the world. The BLN includes libraries, library networks, archives, subject matter experts, online communities and library service providers. We believe every book ever published should be available as a high-quality print reproduction; printed on- demand anywhere in the world. This insures the ongoing accessibility of the content and helps generate sustainable revenue for the libraries and organizations that work to preserve these important materials.

The following book is in the "public domain" and represents an authentic reproduction of the text as printed by the original publisher. While we have attempted to accurately maintain the integrity of the original work, there are sometimes problems with the original book or micro-film from which the books were digitized. This can result in minor errors in reproduction. Possible imperfections include missing and blurred pages, poor pictures, markings and other reproduction issues beyond our control. Because this work is culturally important, we have made it available as part of our commitment to protecting, preserving, and promoting the world's literature.

GUIDE TO FOLD-OUTS, MAPS and OVERSIZED IMAGES

In an online database, page images do not need to conform to the size restrictions found in a printed book. When converting these images back into a printed bound book, the page sizes are standardized in ways that maintain the detail of the original. For large images, such as fold-out maps, the original page image is split into two or more pages.

Guidelines used to determine the split of oversize pages:

• Some images are split vertically; large images require vertical and horizontal splits.
• For horizontal splits, the content is split left to right.
• For vertical splits, the content is split from top to bottom.
• For both vertical and horizontal splits, the image is processed from top left to bottom right.

Price 6d.

THE

LONDON RAMBLER

AND

FOOTPATH GUIDE

TO THE

Surrounding Districts.

BY

HOWARD EVANS.

REPRINTED (WITH ADDITIONS) BY PERMISSION FROM THE
"ECHO."

London:
PUBLISHED BY H. VICKERS, 317, STRAND, W.C.

1881.

Entered at Stationers' Hall.

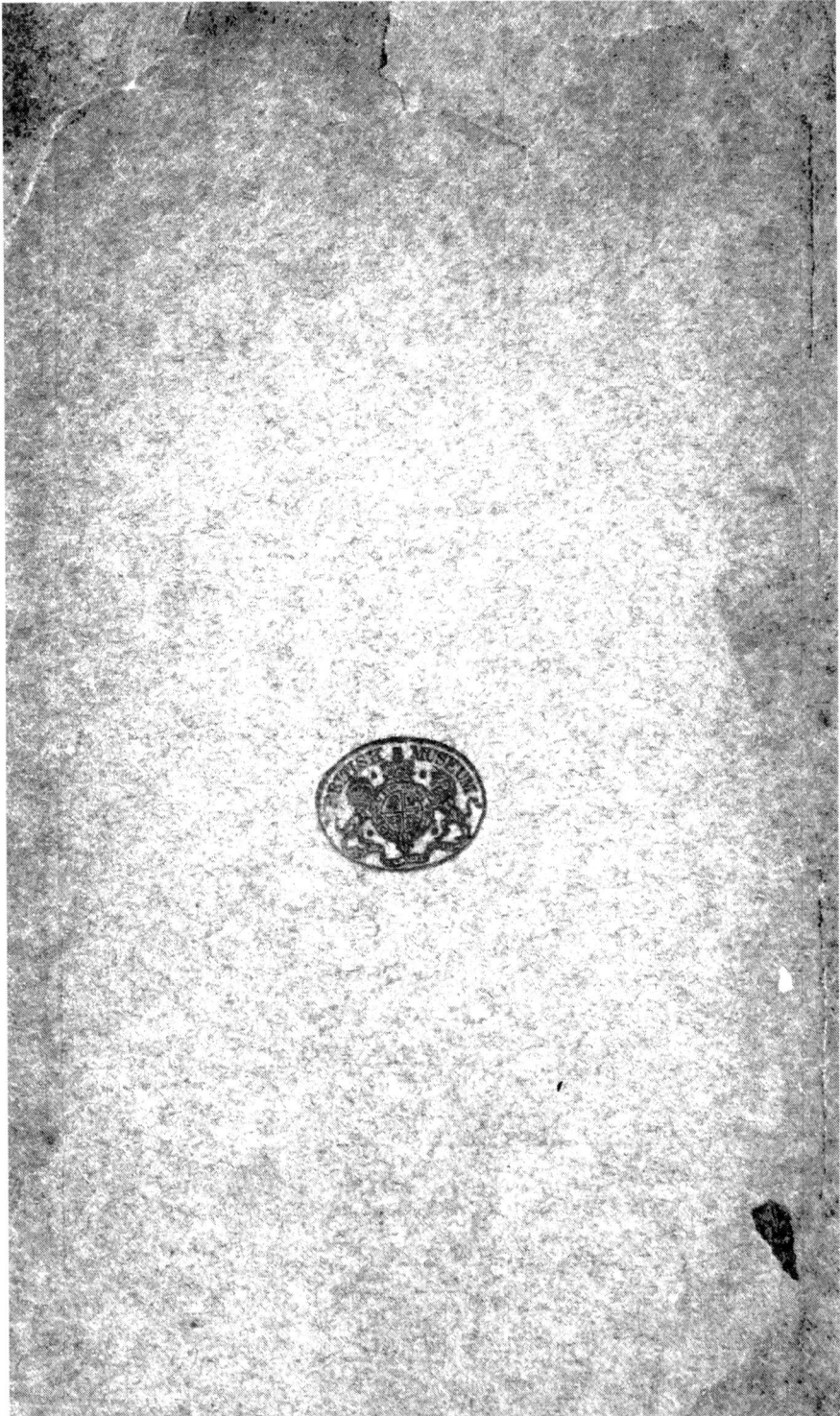

PREFACE.

A S I have no pecuniary interest in the success of this Guide Book, and am not at all likely to make another venture in the same field of literature, I may be permitted to speak of my own work with unwonted freedom. This Guide Book owes its existence to a few suggestions thrown out in an article on Bank Holidays, the substance of which will be found in the first chapter. Certain readers of the said article suggested that it would be advantageous to follow up the subject, and the suggestion was adopted. I can say without boasting that this is as honest a piece of work as I have ever done in my life, and that I have walked hundreds of miles in order to compile it—for I have said nothing of my many walks which ended in disappointment—and have only given the reader that which was worth having. It is not always easy to indicate footpaths on paper, but I have done my best; and I have the satisfaction of knowing that not a few correspondents, strangers as well as personal friends, having followed my directions have expressed their pleasure at the results. The pressure of political and literary work has hitherto hindered the republication of these articles; it has been to me a labour of love to revise and correct them, knowing as I do that they will certainly add to the pure delight of many a humble holiday-maker. Critics will, I hope, be good enough to bear in mind that, though I have occasionally allowed my enthusiasm to break loose, I am not a word-painter but a finger-post; and as a finger-post I must be judged. Throughout last summer I spent most of my leisure hours on a tricycle; and, while it must be admitted that wheels have advantages of their own, my mature judgment inclines to the freedom of footpath rambles. I would not recommend the wayfarer to follow my guidance slavishly if he finds an inviting field-way which I have failed to indicate; for I have frequently experienced the joy of some new discovery which I would not withhold from others. As a rule, it is best not to take a return ticket when starting on a suburban ramble; and the rambler should invariably provide himself with a good map and with a sixpenny railway time-table.

H. E

THE LONDON RAMBLER

By HOWARD EVANS

GENERAL HINTS.

DURING the last few years persistent and successful efforts have been made to secure permanently to Londoners the large open spaces in the outer suburbs, which were in danger of being sacrificed to the builders; but only very partially are they utilised at holiday times and on Saturday afternoons. It seems as though to the vast majority of Londoners the outer suburbs of the Metropolis were still a *terra incognita*. The late Lord Beaconsfield, in a recently published letter, observed that sylvan scenery never palls, and outer London is peculiarly rich in sylvan scenery. It is strange that, with such a wide range of selection, the Londoner's choice of rambles is so limited. As a rule, holiday-makers follow the river: Eastward as far as Southend, Westward as far as Windsor; only a few, with ampler leisure and longer purses, know aught of the beauties of Maidenhead, Cookham, Henley, and Pangbourne. Considering that a broad river will impart beauty to even the tamest scenery, it is but natural that river-side villages should be popular even with those who do not care to blister their soft hands by pulling a scull. The banks of the Thames will always have commanding attractions to a Londoner; but there is no reason why he should confine himself almost exclusively when taking a short holiday ramble, as he does now. With the exception of Epping Forest, and a few rural spots which possess taverns that have acquired some reputation for beanfeasts or for sports of various kinds, there are very few outer suburban villages, away from the banks of the Thames, that have anything like a popular reputation. Even Hendon, Broxbourne, and the Rye House owe

their popularity mainly to the Brent Reservoir and the River Lea.

Let us take the inner circle on the Southern side of the Thames first, in which there are four or five broad, open commons. Only a mile of pleasant rural road separates Tooting Common from Clapham Common; less than a mile of equally pleasant road separates Streatham Common from Tooting Common. Take away the cricketers on a spring Saturday afternoon, and Clapham has its visitors by thousands, Tooting by hundreds, and Streatham by tens. Tooting is flat, like Clapham, and is only superior because it is somewhat more rural, and has finer trees; but Streatham is on the slope of a hill, and its summit commands on two sides views of surpassing loveliness, the valley of verdure westward being at least equal to the well-known view from the terrace on Richmond Hill. If the rambler will cross the common by the single road that bisects it, and opens the latched door at the end of the road, he will find himself, as he pursues his downward way across the fields and over the stiles into the main road, amid secluded scenes of rural beauty that will almost compel him to imagine that he is wandering in some Midland county instead of in a suburb not more than half-a-dozen miles from London Bridge. A sixpenny 'bus fare, or as cheap a railway journey (L.B.S.C.R.), will place him within half-a-mile of this spot; yet on almost any summer afternoon or evening he may find a vacant resting-place on the few seats at the summit of Streatham Common. Equally accessible are the wooded suburban village of Dulwich and the range of hills traversed by the L.C.D.R. line to the Crystal Palace.

There are few Londoners who are not acquainted with the splendid prospect from the garden terrace of the Crystal Palace, but to ninety-nine out of a hundred the heights which they see at a distance are a *terra incognita.* If they would only take the trouble to satisfy themselves they would find the reverse of the picture equally beautiful. That dark brown patch a little to the right, for instance, we will suppose attracts the visitor's attention, and on inquiry he is told that those are the Shirley Hills. After a little inquiry he learns that Shirley is a hamlet not far from Croydon, and he determines that his next pilgrimage in search of beauty shall be a little further afield. Hitherto he has known Croydon only as a stopping place on the road to Brighton or Hastings, or some other Sussex or Kentish watering-place. But Croydon itself is well worth a visit. Croydon is a town of many stations. We will be content to take West Croydon as the least convenient for our purpose, and as the most convenient for transit; it shall be the starting-point for a single afternoon's walk. We include three chief points in a ramble of eight miles; those who are too feeble for such a journey may choose one or two out of the three. Half-a-mile of road and a mile of very stony footpaths will bring the rambler to the Water Tower, situated on elevated ground, at the side of which is a mound covering a reservoir that supplies the lower part of the town with water. From this mound is a charming prospect in almost any direction, the most striking features of which are the wooded hills on Mr. C. Goschen's estate and the dark wood of Croham Hurst, the most southerly point of our excursion. Descending southward from the Water Tower into a main road, and following it some little distance to the left, the traveller comes upon a new avenue on his right, which is being rapidly filled with modern villas, on the summit of which he finds a footpath to the left, that leads him past a farmhouse and through well-tilled fields to the foot of a wooded hill. Climbing the path through the wood, he at last finds himself on the bare summit of Croham Hurst, and a widely-extended prospect meets his view. Far to the right is the high ground of Banstead Downs; nearer is Smitham Bottom; a clump of trees and houses marks Caterham Junction, but the lovely Caterham Valley is hid by intervening hills. Immediately below him is a steep wooded descent. Retracing his steps by the path he came, he comes again to the bottom of the hill, and, keeping a chalk pit in sight, he follows a farm road till he reaches it. Here he will find a finger-post, which directs him to the Shirley Hills.

If he takes the path to Addington he will find himself in the midst of still more romantic beauty; but the path to Shirley itself will satisfy the rural taste of the pedestrian. A mile further and the Shirley Hills are close at hand. The ground is under the control of the Croydon Local Board, but such is its solitude that even on a fine spring Saturday afternoon in May we have seen almost every seat provided for wayfarers empty. The rambler here finds the picture on the Crystal Palace Garden Terrace exactly reversed, and, if possible, he is the gainer by the change of standpoint. The wooded slopes at the back of Shirley and Addington are so unlike anything in the outer Metropolitan suburbs, that he would be amply repaid if they had nothing else to reveal to him; but the view towards Norwood, Sydenham, and Forest Hill is surpassing in its loveliness. The return journey to West Croydon, partly through a leafy avenue of road and partly through field pathways, has a beauty of its own, the whole round being not more than eight or nine miles. At holiday times and on Saturday afternoons our popular places of resort are often inconveniently crowded, while equally attractive spots, as conveniently reached, are quite destitute of visitors, the chief reason being that so few Londoners really know where to go. The cases that we have cited are but a few out of a hundred that might be adduced to show how little many of our choicest open spaces are known and used by the people of the Metropolis.

ELTHAM.

To that great class of Londoners who have neither bicycles, tricycles, horses, gigs, or carriages, whose holidays are mostly half-holidays, who are not overburdened with either money or family cares, who love natural beauty, who care much more for a quiet country lane than for a crowded tavern tea-garden, and, above all, who are not too emasculated to enjoy a walk of a few miles, I venture to offer a few hints on the attractions of our suburbs, and the best way of enjoying them. Whoever will accept my guidance will be good enough to make it a rule to begin and end his ramble at least half-a-dozen miles from home, using railways simply as the means of skipping over the intervening bricks and mortar. I will do my best to lead him by field-paths rather than by hot and dusty roads; but paths are not always easy to indicate. He must supplement paper directions by the use of a good map and his own judgment. Never buy a map that is not cloth-mounted. It will be enough to mention railways without specifying their termini, fares given will be always third class, and to or from the terminus. Those living near intermediate stations can easily calculate the difference.

Let us take for our first centre Eltham, which may be reached by S.E.R. direct for 1s. 6d. return. The City or Westminster rambler may approach it from Woolwich by way of the river; 5d. single, 8d. return. This steamboat trip is the cheapest ride in London; but people who don't care for soldiers and cannons object that there is nothing to see at Woolwich. Let the reader walk to Eltham, four miles distant, across breezy Woolwich Common, and up the road to Shooter's Hill, which is full in sight. Arrived at the hill, on the further side of the main road, he will find a tract of broken ground, from whence he will view a widely-extended prospect, extending from the Crystal Palace to the river. Then let him follow the road over the brow of the hill, and go a few yards up the first turning to the left after the descent begins, when a still more extended prospect towards Erith, Bexley, and Dartford will meet his gaze. Turning back to the summit of the hill, exactly opposite the " Bull," is a narrow road that looks like a carriage-drive. If the rambler does not mind an extra mile or so, let him by all means take that road to Eltham. It soon dwindles into a lumpy, grassy farm road—not to be traversed in wet weather. Delightful woods, with no hideous high fences, are on either side for some distance; then it is wood on one side, and open country on the other. Bye and bye, on the left, there are charming panoramic prospects, and throughout the walk the solitude is unbroken. When the track emerges into a turnpike-road, turning to the right the rambler soon reaches Eltham.

The more direct path from the summit of Shooter's Hill is a few yards from the " Bull," towards London. Here, too, there are woods on either hand, but shut in by tantalising tall fences and walls. These passed, the rambler suddenly emerges upon open meadows with charming prospects in all directions. At the third field he may slant off towards Eltham Church, which is full in sight, or keep straight on by the farm; either way is beautiful. The rambler who has reached Eltham by the way before indicated, to come back this road must start from the churchyard; if he has come by the second path and wants to return by the first, let him take the road to Bexley for a mile, and turn up to the left when he comes to a clump of firs.

There are many ramblers in the South-Eastern suburbs who, either by tram, or by Blackheath Hill Station on the L.C.D.R. line, or by Blackheath Station on the S.E.R. line, will find Blackheath the best starting point for Eltham. The fares are but a few pence either way. Let them avoid the dull, uninteresting highway. The heath has charms of its own, though it be the face of an old familiar friend, and provides soft green turf for the pedestrian from end to end. Once across the heath in the direction of Shooter's Hill, the second turning to the right, Kidbrooke Park Road, after the first quarter of a mile, happily shrinks into a field-path. Eltham Church lies straight ahead, so there is no fear of missing the way, and there is a pleasant and extensive prospect before and behind. I need hardly add that, to vary the return walk, the path described from Eltham Churchyard to Shooter's Hill and home by the road, and across Blackheath, is only a couple of miles further.

Those who live on the L.C.D.R. line will find it pleasant to reach Eltham *via* Bromley (return fare 1s. 5d.) a distance of between four and five miles, field-path nearly all the way. At the station ask for Love Lane, at the end of which, crossing the road, inquire for the path to Plastow Place—a point, by the way, which can be also reached from Beckenham Station by turning to the left till the Ravensbourne is crossed, then to the right, and up the first field-path on the right, and the first field-path on the right again, through a glorious park, and so to Plastow. Here a finger-post indicates the field-path to Mottingham and Eltham, the sylvan beauties of which I cannot stay to describe. Discarding all roads, right or left, the rambler should keep on this track till it ends in

a main road. Then turning to the right for a short distance down the hill, he will find a little gate on the left
that leads him across a railway to the chief attraction of
Eltham. He need not return the same way, but, inquiring at Eltham for the path to Kidbrooke Church, he will
continue his walk to Blackheath; and at Blackheath Hill
he is once more in his own line again.

Familiar as I am with all these various ways, I would
recommend as the best the steamboat trip to Woolwich,
the walk to Shooter's Hill, by the wood path exactly
opposite the " Bull " to Eltham, round the back of King
John's Palace, across the line into a turnpike-road, up
that road to the right till the first narrow turning to the
left is reached, and so across to Plastow and Bromley—
in all about ten miles.

And now a word on the chief attraction of Eltham.
It is but a stone's throw out of the main street of
the village, approached by a road that has a row
of fine trees on the one side, and behind them certain quaint old cottages. Then the rambler reaches an
ancient Gothic bridge, across which once rode our
Plantagenet, Yorkist, and Lancastrian Kings. The
bridge spans a moat which now exists on one side of the
palace only. The moat is bordered by a smooth level of
grassy sward, and the sloping banks are covered with
foliage. Flanking the bridge on either hand is an ancient
house, in which dwell certain Government officials. In
front is the ancient Banquetting Hall, where not a few
of the Kings of England used to keep their Christmas.
The hall is of stone, with a red-tiled roof, its style of
architecture resembling Crosby Hall; the arrangement
of the windows, now partially bricked up, being not
unlike those of the House of Commons. At the extreme
end the fan-work tracery in the interior of the great
windows indicates work of a Tudor age, though the rest
of the building is much older. To the left of the old
hall, and apparently a portion of the ancient building,
though the front has been restored, is an inhabited house,
the further half of which, with its gabled roof and barge
boards, seems to indicate that it belongs at least to the
sixteenth century. " Our Royal Palace at Eltham " was
the residence of Henry III., Edward I., II., III.,

Richard II·, Henry IV., V., Edward IV., Henry VI. and VIII., the last of whom, however, conceived a preference for Greenwich. Eltham has been the residence at times of not a few distinguished persons, including Sir W. Roper and Margaret his wife, daughter of Sir Thomas More, Vandyck the painter, and Sherard the botanist. Those who are anxious to know more of the palace must turn to the county histories. I am quite content if by one field-path or another I shall be able to beckon some London ramblers to the Gothic bridge over the ancient moat, where they will find one of the most charming pictures of old-world life that can be found within walking distance of the Metropolis.

CROYDON.

THE more I see of the outer suburbs, the more convinced am I that, as a rule, the wealthier residents desire that such as myself shall confine ourselves to dusty highways. I should very much like to put up finger-posts at both ends of all the field-paths and bridle-ways that I know. Mr. Crœsus, of Crœsus Brothers & Co., Lombard Street, on the contrary, selects his eligible site, the entrance to which is, perhaps, a few yards down an ancient bridle-way or green lane, and proceeds to erect his mansion. He does not shut us out, but he levels the lane and gravels it; perhaps he puts up a gate, which is, of course, left open; perhaps he builds a lodge hard by. Mr. Crœsus is wide awake enough to know that so deferential are we to the rights of property that the lodge, the gate, even the gravel alone is quite as effective in keeping us off as though a board was stuck up with the lying legend, " Trespassers " will be prosecuted with the utmost rigour of the law." Did you ever know a trespasser prosecuted with the utmost rigour of the law unless he was in pursuit of game or did some specific damage ? If your intentions are innocent the worst that will happen is that you will find yourself in a *cul de sac* or be warned off by a gamekeeper.

As the chief attractions of Croydon lie south or east of the town, the rambler should take the rail to Croydon direct—return fares 1s. 3d. and 1s. 6d. Tickets taken for West Croydon are available for the return journey from

East Croydon, but not by all trains. For Shirley and Addington, East Croydon is better than West; Addiscombe Road nearer still. For Croham Hurst, South Croydon is nearest. We will take West Croydon for a first starting point. Inquire for the Parish Church, at the back of which are interesting remains of the old Archiepiscopal Palace. Passing out of the churchyard at the far end through an ancient stone gateway, the rambler will find a steep path almost opposite him. At the end of this a short road brings him to Duppas Hill, a fine open space, with extensive views, east, west, and south. Before him on the left is Hayling Park, skirting which is a path that, after passing the park, leads him through open fields up the gradual ascent of Russell Hill. Near the asylum there is a commanding prospect in every direction: eastward, beyond Addington, is Shooter's Hill; westward, Banstead Downs; northward, the hills of Sydenham, Norwood and Streatham; and far away to the north-west is the faint outline of Harrow-on-the-Hill. At the asylum the pretty valley of Caterham begins to open out. If the rambler is already tired of his three-mile journey, he may return to Croydon from Caterham Junction Station; otherwise let him turn up the main road towards Croydon for half-a-mile till he reaches a group of houses, where he will find a road to the right, which in two or three minutes brings him to the grand old patriarchal oaks of Purley. It was here that the sturdy patriot Horne Tooke wrote his well-known "Diver-" sions of Purley." Proceeding up the road for a short distance, the rambler reaches the green heights of Purley Downs, covered with juniper bushes, from which the view is very similar to that on the opposite eminence of Russell Hill. Keeping straight forward across the turf he will come once more into a lane leading to a high road. Immediately before him is a delightful wood. Bearing to the right, either through the wood or by the road, he will soon find himself at Sanderstead Church. To the left of the churchyard is a lane that leads through another charming wood, on the side of the hill. Thence across open fields the rambler comes to the foot of the steep ascent of Croham Hurst. At the summit he will pause to rest and to admire the wide and varied prospect before

him.   Descending on the other side, through the woods,
he will find his way mainly by footpaths to the Water
Tower, and thence by footpaths again into Croydon Town.
The whole distance is about ten miles.   I have been
assured, though I have never seen it myself, that from
the summit of Croham Hurst, the Round Tower of
Windsor is, on a clear day, distinctly visible.

The route above described is rather too long for a
lovers' walk; let us next take a shorter one.   From
George Street, near both the East and West Croydon
Stations, is a path that leads up to the Water Tower.   It
is well to go right up to the tower for the view on the
mound by the side of it, and then return by the same way
till the rambler comes to a path on the right, which leads
across a new road, and over a hill into Combe Lane—an
arid road, but sheltered by umbrageous trees, as are most
roads in this neighbourhood.   A mile or two brings the
rambler to the Shirley and Addington Hills.   Let him
leave the road and climb up a little to the left, when he
will find a magnificent prospect before him.   He may
ramble on over the heather-covered heights till he strikes
into a road which descends the hills, and, winding to the
left through the lower ground, with splendid park-like
scenery on either hand, brings him back by way of
Addington to Croydon again.   This round involves only
about five or six miles of walking.

If this distance is too short, instead of proceeding
along the hills, when he has satisfied himself with the
prospect, let the rambler come back to the road again and
descend it towards Croydon, till he comes to a finger-post
which indicates the footpath to Selsdon.   As he descends
he will find beautiful woodlands on his left and far-
reaching prospects on his right, till he comes to a finger-
post, which indicates a bridle-way to Addington.   Southward is open country; on the other side are magnificent
pine woods, till the path emerges into a main-road, which
will lead him, if he turns to the right, to Addington
Village.

For some distance before reaching the village he has
been skirting the noble park of the Archbishop of Canterbury, on whose wooded slopes he has doubtless looked

if 'Arry and 'Arriet, with a dozen companions, burst upon
this quiet spot, adorned with paper streamers and roaring
out the chorus of "To 'Ampstead in a wan," they would
find it inaccessible; Jim Moleskin, the poacher, attracted
by the rabbits, would no doubt also find his room preferable to his company. But as a matter of favour I do
not think that there is much difficulty as regards entrance.
Such at any rate is my own experience. I was told by a
respectable Addingtonian that if I went through the farm
opposite the village inn I should meet with no obstruction,
and, accompanied by a friend, I ventured in. Twice I
inquired of men employed in the grounds near the palace
if I could go that way towards Croydon, and was politely
directed on the road. At the lodge gate where I emerged
a woman came out with a key, but asked no questions.
I take it that the Archbishop intends to show Christian
courtesy to harmless wayfarers who have no other object
but to enjoy natural beauty, and thank him accordingly
for the opportunity of roaming through one of the most
picturesque domains in the vicinity of London.

There is one exception to the rule against approaching Croydon by intervening stations, and that is Beckenham. It is possible to go to Croydon from that suburban
L.C.D.R. station for the most part by footpaths or woodland lanes where the ground is as soft as a Turkey carpet.
From the station, past Beckenham Church, let the rambler
follow the Wickham Road for about two miles and a half;
most of the way the road skirts a park with shading trees
on the right. At last he will come to a round lodge with
thatched roof on the right hand. His turning point is a
yard or two further on the same side. Through pleasant
woodlands and meadows he proceeds till he emerges on
the main road. Turning to the right, past a pond, let
him look out for the first turning on the left, through an
open gate. He will recognise it, because just beyond is
a lodge with four pine logs for its miniature portico.
Thence for a mile or so, through leafy woodlands on
either hand, his velvet pathway leads him over a hill to
Addington Village. If he is too timid to attempt an
entrance to the park itself, when he gets to the top of
the hill, before descending it into Addington Village, he
will find to his right a road skirting the park, and a

charming road it is, which, if steadily pursued, will bring
him by way of Shirley Church into the Addiscombe Road,
and so to Croydon.

The following is a very pleasant walk of six miles.
Starting from Croydon take the road to Shirley; when
near Shirley take the Shirley Church Road on the left,
which the rambler cannot miss if he can read. After
passing the church and school the road skirts the Archbishop's park, the sylvan scenery of which is delightful.
At the end of the road follow the bridle-path straight
forward through Wickham Woods, on emerging from
which the rambler finds West Wickham a few yards on
the left. There is a station of the S.E.R. at this village.

Residents in Anerley, Penge, and Norwood will find
the Shirley and Addington Hills accessible enough without resorting to railways at all. They will, however,
miss half their beauty if they are simply contented to
climb the bare hills, recently planted by the Croydon
Board of Health with young trees, and content themselves with the beauty of the noble prospect northward.
At the back of the hills is a dark wood of pines, whose
hard straight lines produce upon the visitor the same
solemn effect which comes over him as he gazes on the
afterglow in a summer evening. There is something
peculiarly attractive, too, in the sylvan scenery beyond.
It is unlike anything else to be seen in suburban London.
Among the sombre pines the silver stems of the birches
and the "living green" of the young larches have a
delightful effect.

It may be worthy of mention, for the benefit of
Sunday ramblers, that at Addington and Shirley the
chief village inns have but a six-day licence.

BROMLEY.

For parks and woodlands there is no place at an equal
distance from London that surpasses Bromley, which is
reached by the S.E.R. and L.C. & D.R. (single 8½d.,
return 1s. 5d.) The latter line has three stations in the
valley—Shortlands, Bromley, and Bickley—from either
of which delightful excursions may be made. We will
take Shortlands as our first starting point. On leaving

the station and crossing the stream, the road, by a steep ascent, brings the rambler to the northern end of the little town, where he will turn to the left. The large old-fashioned building on his right is a college for clergyman's widows. Following the road for some little distance let him turn to the right by the side of the cemetery, and keeping straight forward with a park fence on the left hand he will by and bye see a stile through which he may pass into the park, which possesses a quiet rural beauty that will repay him for the slight deviation from his track. Returning to the road let him follow it till four cross-roads are reached, one of which, indicated on the finger-post, is the road to Chislehurst. Following this road let the rambler keep a look-out for a path on the left. From this another path deviates to the left, but we will keep along the higher ground through a corn-field, and thence into the beautiful wooded park of Sundridge. Soft, undulating pasture lies before us, and beyond a range of hills crowned with verdure. Not even Richmond nor Windsor can present a fairer scene. At the end of the path, through a lodge gate, we emerge into the road, on the opposite side of which is another path through woodland and fields. Passing under the railway arch we find another path on the left, climbing up the hill, which leads us through the park of Camden Place, with a view of the back of the house, whence we emerge at last upon Chislehurst Common. Almost opposite the gates of Camden Place he will see a road leading underneath an archway. A short distance down he will see Chislehurst Station (S.E.R.) a little to the right, by which he can return to town (9d. single). Following the road under the railway a walk of two miles will bring him to Bickley (fare to town the same). If he does not mind four or five miles more on foot, he may take the route hereinafter indicated, by St. Paul's Cray Common ; or finally he may go back through the path by whence he emerged, and strike into another path that passes through the lower ground, which at last brings him into a lane leading to the lower end of Chislehurst. Crossing the main road, he will find another lane, which, after a little while, bears off to the left, from whence he will have commanding views of the surrounding country, which will amply compensate for the stony character of the way. Just after crossing the railway a path to the left brings him to Eltham Station (fare to town, 9d). If this route is taken, the rambler will, of course, take the opportunity of visiting Eltham Palace, described in a previous chapter. In this, as in other chapters, I have endeavoured to indicate the best routes for several afternoon rambles ; but I would recommend the walk through Sundridge Park, from Shortlands or Bromley, to Chislehurst as the most attractive, because, while it is so surpassing in its beauty, it requires so little road travelling, and is so short as to be within the powers of almost any pedestrian.

The rambler may find a shorter, though not quite so pleasant, a way to Chislehurst by road. From Bromley the S.E.R. station is nearer than the L.C. & D.R., and the road is straight. If starting from the L.C. & D.R. station, turn up Love Lane—a path just beyond the station on the left. After ascending some little distance, a gate on the right leads into a footpath that leads across the park of the late Mr. Coles Child, which contains some grand old trees. After passing through the park, a turning to the left will bring the rambler into the main road, which he will not regret to reach, for he will have had enough of those black pebbles which are the plague of so many bye-roads in West Kent. Arrived at Chislehurst Common, just before reaching the Prince Imperial's monument are certain cross-roads. Let him take that leading to St. Mary Cray. After a short walk he will observe on the right a narrow turning between two rows of houses, which brings him to the little Catholic church where lie the remains of Napoleon III. and his son. Turning to the left the rambler will soon reach St. Paul's Cray Common, whose beauty is almost equal to that of Chislehurst, though of a far different order. The first road track slanting off to the right will bring him to a lane through delightful woodlands. On some of the trees right and left are notices warning off trespassers, but, as there is nothing at the entrance of the lane, I presume that they are intended only to warn pedestrians not to deviate from the track. At the far end are gates crossing a line of railway. Crossing this the lane passes between open fields, with occasional long-distance views of the wooded country eastward. Another railway is crossed, and finally the lane strikes into another. The left-hand road leads to Orpington (three miles), where there is a S.E.R. station. Let us turn to the right, following the windings of the lane till a little brown house faces us. Do not proceed further, for at the house the lane ceases, and, though there is a style into a footpath skirting a wood, the path leads nowhere. So when the little brown house is in sight look out for a footpath on the left. Following this for some distance across the fields the little hamlet of Southbro' is reached. Here, just beyond the cross-roads, is a swing-gate leading into a path across level meadows, on emerging from which, the first turning to the left and the second to the right brings the rambler to Bickley Station, L.C.& D.R. This round is not far short of a dozen miles.

Hitherto our excursions have been east of Bromley, but the country southward is quite as attractive. Leaving the train at Shortlands, let us take the path on the right by the side of the stream, which soon brings us to St. Martin's Hill, a public recreation ground, from the top of which are charming, if not very extensive, views. The churchyard, a few yards down the road at the back of the hill, is well worth a visit; it is entered by the second gate. Returning to St. Martin's Hill, let us follow the path down the slope on the left. Turning to the left by the side of the stream a little way, a footpath crosses the railway and ascends the opposite slope, slanting across several fields, until a road is reached. Exactly opposite is another path by the side of a wall, which follow till a new road is crossed, when a path will be seen opposite, leading through a wood of young oaks, only passable in dry weather. On emerging through a gate into the road, the rambler who only desires a short walk may turn to the right and find his way back to Shortlands.

Those who are not afraid of a walk of a dozen miles in all will turn to the left, through a delightfully umbrageous road, that leads by way of Pickhurst Green to Hayes. Just before reaching the village he has to turn sharp off to the right; then the first to the left brings

him to Hayes Common. Let him follow the Keston
Road. Perhaps he will wonder at first why this spot has
been so highly praised; he will wonder no longer when
he arrives at the other end and turns round to gaze upon
one of the loveliest prospects which his eyes have ever
seen. The whole range of the Sydenham Hills is before
him, to the right are the wooded hills of Bromley and
Chislehurst, beyond is Shooter's Hill, and in the extreme
distance are the hills of Essex. Londoners who have
never visited Hayes will be amply rewarded by doing so
on the first leisure afternoon. But a very short distance
after passing Hayes Common the road enters Keston
Common, thickly covered with heather and furze, where
opens a grand view on the right, which has hitherto been
hidden. About fifty yards past the windmill a path
slants to the left across the common, which brings the
rambler to a swing-gate that leads into Holwood Park,
whose sylvan beauties have so often been described that
they need no lengthened reference here. Following the
path for some distance the rambler may take his well-
earned rest on the stone seat which marks the spot where
Wilberforce held a conversation with Pitt which resulted
in his giving notice in the House of Commons of a motion
for the Abolition of the Slave Trade. If the rambler
pursues the path down the hill till he reaches the road,
turning to the left for a few miles, he will find himself
at Orpington Station, upon the S.E.R., but the probability is that he will have been so delighted with the
way which he has travelled that he will be content to
return by the same road as far as the village of Hayes,
where he will find a station from which he can return to
town by the S.E.R.

WIMBLEDON.

WIMBLEDON offers such a happy combination of near and
distant landscape scenery, that we may say with truth
that no spot on the southern side of the Thames, so close
to London, possesses such varied and charming views.
Mere birds of passage on the L. & S.W. line, or casual
visitors to the annual Rifle Competition, can have but a
faint idea of its beauty, abounding as it does with

" places of nestling green, for poets made." The station (S.W.R., fare 7d., return 1s. 2d.) is about a mile from the common. It may be reached by rail from London Bridge, Ludgate Hill, and Victoria, as well as from Waterloo. A South London rambler may take the train to Clapham Road, or a car to the common, and will find a pleasant walk of four miles each way. Crossing the commn, with the Balham Road only a few yards to the left, at the far end, he will reach Nightingale Lane, at the other end of which is Wandsworth Common. Keeping the line of the road straight forward, some distance after passing the common he will come to a road at right angles; bearing to the left he will at last cross the Wandel, which, by the way, is now nowhere a picturesque stream, save at its source at Carshalton. The road gradually ascends after crossing the bridge, and on turning the rambler will find that it commands a pretty view of the country behind him, and of the more distant Surrey heights south-ward. After passing a new cemetery, just where the road bends to the left he will come to an open lodge-gate. By no means miss this, for it is the entrance to Wimbledon Park, in which have been recently erected some noble suburban residences—happily but a few as yet. The road is private, but visitors are allowed to pass through, though they are not permitted to stray into the contiguous woods and grounds. No one need deviate from the track whose eye can be satisfied with a delight-ful combination of wood and water. Down in a verdant little valley close in front is an extensive lake, and beyond it richly wooded heights close in the scene. It is difficult to realise in the midst of all this sequestered sylvan beauty that the visitor is but eight miles from Bow Bells. In but a few years the suburban villa will be monarch of this noble domain; but while yet its beauty remains unmarred the opportunity of visiting it should not be lost. The road leaves the park close by the church, and if the rambler turns to the left, and follows the road till he comes to the gate by which he first entered, he will find noble prospects of the Banstead and Epsom Downs and other Surrey eminences on his way. It is worthy of notice that this beautiful estate has been held in turn by Queen Henrietta Maria ;. Lambert, Cromwell's Lieutenant ; Digby, Earl of Bristol ;. the first Duke of Leeds ; Sarah, Duchess of Marlborough ;. and the first Lord Spencer.

Let us now start to Wimbledon by rail direct, and, leaving the station, turn up to the common. We strike off sharp to the left across the common by a road that cuts off its extreme corner, and, reaching the houses at the end, we follow the road skirting the common till we find only a style straight before us. Pausing for a moment to admire the wooded heights of Richmond Park we cross the stile, and at once turn off to the left by a soft grassy track, which skirts a wood where Mr. Alphabet Drax threatens what he will do to trespassers. Strolling some little distance along this pleasant bye-way we come to a stile on the left which slants across a field. At the end of this field take the footpath to the right, which, after crossing a small brook, ascends the opposite slope, at first skirting a wood, and ultimately passing through it. On reaching a lane with some red-brick buildings opposite we turn to the right, and soon emerge upon three main roads, one of which leads to Malden S.W.R. station, which is not far off, fare 9d. I would specially recommend this ramble, because it not only commands delightful views, but is green lane, common, or footpath for three parts of the distance.

If the walk is not long enough, on reaching the three roads above-mentioned we will take the one to the left, which commands extensive panoramic views southward of a wide valley and of the Downs in the distance. On reaching a little bridge we look out for a footpath on the left across level meadows, and on once more striking into a road we turn to the left again, till, after ascending some distance, we find another field-path on the left, which we take. All the way the prospect on either hand is charming, but just when the path emerges into the road once more let the rambler pause to look down the the miniature wooded dell, with the hills round Kingston closing in the view. On re-entering the road turn to the left, and a short walk brings us to Wimbledon once more. This round will not be much beyond six miles, and less than half the distance is along high roads.

Those who prefer a two or three miles longer ramble, on reaching the common should strike across it in the direction of the flagstaff till they come upon the Kingston Road. Following the road for a mile or two, on the right is the Robin Hood Gate leading into Richmond Park, a pleasure ground whose beauties are little known to Londoners, save the green slope at the Petersham Gate and the entrance at Richmond Hill. On entering at the Robin Hood Gate keep the line of the middle road straigt across the park till two large ponds are in sight. Then leave the road and take to the grassy track between the two, and so straight forward across the grass till the Richmond Gate is in sight. On leaving the park at Richmond Hill, pass the " Star and Garter," and, after enjoying the well-known view from the Terrace, turn down the field to the left into the lower road. A few yards to the right along this road is a way leading to the waterside, which may be pursued under Richmond Bridge; then taking the first turning to the right, the rambler reaches Richmond Green, crossing which in a slanting direction he will find himself close to Richmond Station : S.W.R. fare, 9d. Trains will also take him to Broad Street and Ludgate Hill.

Hitherto we have glanced at the surroundings of Wimbledon to the east and west. The road from the north, *via* Putney Pier or Station (S.W.R.), is too direct to need remark. To the south-west towards Surbiton, and to the south-east towards Croydon, the country is flat and uninteresting, but the rambler due south will be well repaid for his trouble. On leaving Wimbledon Station let us take the road to Lower Merton. The dulness of Merton, by the way, is not a little relieved by some of its quaint old ivy-covered residences. We will turn up the road crossing a railway on a level, and follow it until we reach " The Leather Bottle." A little further on the left is a modern house called " Ellerslie," and just beyond it a lane up which we will turn. This lane affords us pleasant glimpses of the villa-dotted Wimbledon slopes, and at length it strikes along the edge of a park, beyond which we have nothing more than a stile and a footpath along gently sloping meadows, with fair prospects of the country beyond. When we reach a new-made road we turn to the left, and at the end turn to the left again, through Lower Morden. On emerging into a main road we turn to the left once more, and take the first lane to the right, which is shaded nearly the whole distance by lofty elms. The first lane to the right again, a grass track, bounded on either hand by high hedges and trees, and bearing the appropriate name of Love Lane, is well worth a visit in dry weather. At the end turn to the left, and the road will bring you to the beginning of the long, straggling village of Sutton, at the far side of which is a station (L.B.& S.C.R.), fare 1s. 1d. Better, perhaps, having explored this lane, to return by it, and follow the road we came by till we come in sight of a magnificent prospect to the north and east, while, westward, a bosky screen shields us from the rays of the afternoon sun. The heights of Streatham, Norwood, and Sydenham are now full in view; Croydon is in the middle distance; and beyond it the Addington Hills, Croham Hurst, the Purley Downs, and Russell Hill. If the rambler is not yet tired he may descend into the wooded village of Carlshalton, where the clear bright waters of the Wandle add much to the beauty of the scene. There for a shilling the L.B.& S.C.R. will convey him back either to Victoria or London Bridge. The distance from Wimbledon to Carshalton by the route indicated will be about seven miles.

HARROW.

WE Londoners often talk about wanting "a change." We must needs seek the seacoast or the mountains if we need a thorough change of air; but we could not have a more complete change of scene than is to be found ten miles north of the Marble Arch. The sight and the sound of the sea waves, the swift torrents, the bare rocky precipices, are sometimes suggestive of the rush and roar of city life. For our eyes the greatest change is that which is suggestive of complete repose. You may find such a scene from the summit of Malvern, looking eastward over the Severn Valley; or from the Dunstable Downs, looking westward over the Vale of Aylesbury; or from Leith Hill, looking southward over the Weald of Sussex; or from the ridge of Edge Hill, in Warwickshire; but not one of these surpasses the calm beauty of the landscape at the churchyard of Harrow on a summer's evening. Three lines of Tennyson describe it with exquisite fitness—

> " Dewy pastures, dewy trees,
> Softer than sleep—all things in order stored
> A haunt of ancient peace."

Of all seasons of the year, this, the spring, the best for visiting the rich pasture lands of Middlesex, when the level meads are resplendent with shining gold; and of all the northern heights of London the isolated hill of Harrow is the best vantage-ground. Western Middlesex, as you travel across it, seems tame and unattractive, but from this Mount Pisgah its sweet loveliness is inexpressibly soothing to the weary heart and brain. Here, quite as much as on Skiddaw or Cader Idris, we may realise Keble's words:—

> " Lone Nature feels that she may freely breathe,
> And round us and beneath
> Are heard her sacred tones."

From the summit of this verdant hill it is said that no fewer than thirteen counties are visible, though, looking from various points, I can only recognise nine or ten— Middlesex, Herts, Oxon, Bucks, Berks, Hants, Surrey, Kent, and possibly Beds and Essex. Looking from the churchyard straightforward, a little below the last faint outline of the Berkshire Hills is Windsor Castle; a little to the right of this are the Nettlebed Hills, in Oxfordshire; still further to the right the wooded hills of Hertfordshire; and in a gap beyond an eminence which I imagine must be the Dunstable Downs. From the eastern side of the churchyard there are glimpses of the country beyond, but they are much obscured by the modern school buildings which have been recently erected.

Harrow may be reached either by the L.N.W.R. or the Metropolitan (single 10d., return 1s. 3d.); the latter station being the more convenient, we choose it for our starting point. On emerging from the station road to the main road the rambler may turn either up the hill to the left or ot the right. The former route leads him through delightful woodland to the churchyard; but he had better take the footpath which he will see on his right a few yards along this road, because as he ascends the slope he will

find on turning round that it presents a fine view to the
north-east which the churchyard terrace does not give.
The latter road, taking the first turning to the left, will
give him, as he ascends, a pleasant view of the hill itself.
By either route he will soon reach the terrace on the
churchyard, from whence his delighted eyes will gaze upon
the view above described. The western gateway of the
church is Norman, and was in all probability erected in
the time of Lanfranc, who held the See of Canterbury in
the days of William the Conqueror. The interior is ancient,
but there have been extensive restorations. Passing out
of the lych-gate of the churchyard, let us keep straight
forward along the High Street till we pass the Public Hall.
Then we will take the first turning to the left, which,
though unpromising at first, soon presents to us on the one
side a richly-wooded slope, and on the other an extended
view eastward. The last house on the left upon the road,
barred by a modern gate, is well worthy of notice, although
it is modern. So exquisite is its workmanship that it is
more like the labour of a skilled cabinet-maker than of a
bricklayer. Turning back we soon find a narrow passage
on the left that brings us again into the main road. To
the left again we soon reach the brow of the hill, from
whence we look southward across the cloud of London
smoke to the hills of Surrey. We will now turn back
through Harrow, keeping along the main road till we
reach the College Chapel, behind which is a charming
landscape bounded by the high road of Hampstead.
Following the road a little further we reach Peterborough
Road, just after entering which is a footpath to the right
down the slope. Here is the best prospect of Harrow
itself. We follow the path across the meadows till a high
road is reached. Opposite is another path, which passes
through pleasant meadows for a mile, but as it leads nowhere we will turn up the road to the left, till we come to
a path that leads us once more up the Harrow slope.
When the rambler passes out of this path into the road
once more, he may see beyond the smoke of London the
faint outline of the Palace of Sydenham. Thus far I have
written for those who are content to return from the same
station. It may be worth while to add that Harrow is not
a place that lays itself out for the reception of humble

holiday-makers. Those to whom beer in a garden, or tea and shrimps at ninepence, are indispensable, had better keep away from it.

There are many who, like myself, prefer to leave off at a considerable distance from the point where they started. I will offer them two routes almost equally attractive. The rambler will, of course, have followed my directions as to Harrow itself, as given above, till he reaches the foot-path leading out of Peterborough Road. He will follow that path till he reaches the main road, when he will turn to the right. Though he hate high roads, as I do, he must at least admit that it is pleasantly shaded in the afternoon. The first lane on the left, which for a considerable distance possesses the advantage of a grassy footway on either side, skirts the green woodlands of Wembly Park, after passing which the rambler will take the first turning to the right, the second to the left, and the first to the right again. Throughout the whole of this walk the prospect is not extensive, but very pleasant and secluded, towards the end with occasional glimpses of the shining waters of the Brent reservoir. Of this extensive sheet of water I am bound honestly to say that distance lends enchantment to the view; those of us who are acquainted with the clear, bright waters of Bala or Windermere when close upon its banks, cannot fail to make disadvantageous comparisons. But there are thousands of Londoners to whom it will convey a very favourable idea of a lake if they will only ignore the urban name of reservoir, and forget that it owes its existence to the embankment constructed by a canal company. Mr. Warner has utilised its waters and made it a popular London resort. The rambler, having travelled thus far about half-a-dozen miles from Harrow, if he is not tired, may take a row or a sail amid very pretty rural scenery, and afterwards he will find the Welsh Harp Station close at hand, and Hendon Station, both on the Midland (fare 7d. to St. Pancras and 8d. to Moorgate Street), not a mile distant.

The second route I indicate is preferable, because it is green lane or footpath the greater part of the way; but a good walker who does not mind fourteen miles might easily combine both by making Hendon Station his starting-point. On leaving that station he would turn to the right into the main road, when, turning to the left, he would strike off to the right just before reaching the " Upper Welsh Harp." Thence to Harrow he has simply to reverse the directions above given till he reaches Harrow. Having passed through the village along the main road, a little distance beyond the public hall, just beyond the brow of the hill a green lane that apparently leads nowhere is straight before us on the right. It is only a green grassy track, with fragrant hedges of May blossom on either hand; but let us follow it. They call it Love Lane, appropriately enough, for after a lengthened green footway it at last leads into a straight, hard road, which may fitly represent matrimony. Thus we arrive at a distance of three miles from Harrow, to the rustic little village of Northolt. On the rising ground to the left is the quaint old church. Passing through the churchyard we shall find to the right a swing-gate that leads us through verdant meadows, across a canal, and thence across verdant meadows again to the diminutive rustic church of Greenford. Turning down the main road to the right we shall find a lane on the left, which soon leads us to a bewildering meeting of roads and streams. Here let the rambler look for a rustic hostelry, bearing the sign of " The Load of Hay." Turning down past this house he will find a footpath across undulating meadows, with the church of Hanwell full in sight. Here, as at intervals all along the way, he will catch pleasant glimpses behind him of the wooded slopes of Harrow; nor can he fail, as he approaches the churchyard, to be charmed by the gentle woodland scenery of Hanwell itself. Crossing the road just beyond the churchyard he will find another footpath, which leads him to Hanwell Station. From this point a fare of eightpence to Paddington or elevenpence to Victoria will bring him back to town again without the irksome disadvantages of pursuing his way on foot amid modern bricks and mortar.

CHINGFORD.

WITH the exception of one particular spot, I am free to confess that I have no great admiration for Epping Forest *qua* forest. As a playground it is magnificent, though it contains many and many an acre of tangled impenetrable thicket; but, as a forest, it is for the most part a failure, despite all the extravagant eulogies that have been lavished upon it of late. Bush would be the more correct designation for most of it. Chang, the Chinese giant, might almost look right over it if he stood on tip-toe. It is not the fault of Nature. If people will periodically pollard the trees, what chance can the trees have? Let those grow enthusiastic who can over a bunch of leaves on a pole, I own that I cannot. Nevertheless the forest has attractive charms, owing mainly to its elevated situation, and towards its northern extremity, where no sacrilegious hands have lopped the trees, its sylvan beauty is exquisite. At Ching-ord Station, G.E.R. (return 1s.), the visitor is set down close to the forest; and if it is his purpose to explore the forest only, he would do well to purchase a capital sixpenny guide-book at the Liverpool Street bookstall.

Purposely we will take the unpromising starting point of Angel Road Station, G,E.R. (single 7d.), amid the marshes of the lazy Lea. The prospect around us is dull and uninteresting, and the low range of hills before us as we turn eastward looks little more attractive. By and bye a footpath strikes up the hill to the left, and when we turn to look back, just before entering the old churchyard, the far-extended landscape delights us all the more because it comes upon us with surprise. In the middle distance is the dead level of the Lea Marshes, disfigured here and there with gasworks and tall chimneys; but beyond are Highgate, Muswell Hill, and the whole of north-eastern Middlesex. Passing into the churchyard we pause to examine the ivy-covered ruinous old church, which no visitor to Chingford should miss, and then entering the high road, which commands the same fair prospect, we follow it till the first road to the right is reached, descending a hill, a delicious bit of leafy roadway. Turning up a lane opposite the " Fountain," we take the first lane to the left, which soon dwindles to a footpath that leads into a wood (Bury and Hawk Wood). This is one of the most delightful portions of the forest, for the trees are close and thick, yet there is no bewildering tangled undergrowth to impede our progress. Following the wood almost in a straight line from the point where we entered we at last reach a lane; then, turning to the right, we soon are in sight of the New Hotel, by the side of Queen Elizabeth's Lodge, near which is a broad green track to the left that winds through the forest towards High Beech. On emerging into a road the higher ground and nobler trees are full in sight. Unquestionably this is by far the most attractive part of the forest, and the point which every visitor should make for, whether he reaches the district by the Chingford or Loughton Stations. We can wander at our own sweet will beneath the arching boughs of the grand old oaks and beeches, keeping the road within sight, till at length we reach the King's Oak, where the prospect of the surrounding country is most imposing. We must not, however, be satisfied with the view in front of the house westward, but go some little distance behind it for the eastward outlook. Returning to the inn we take the road immediately facing it, which descends the hill rapidly; and when we reach the hill at the bottom, if we turn to the left, we shall find but a few yards on the right hand a stile and a footpath. The path leads across field after field, with pleasant views of the hill country we have just left, almost to Waltham. On entering a lane we keep forward in the same direction; and just past the cemetery another path will bring us straight into Waltham, about eight miles from our starting point.

I might here suggest that Waltham and High Beech might be easily combined in a half-holiday. Waltham Station, G.E.R. (single 1s. 1d.; return, 1s. 7d.), is a mile east of Waltham Abbey. After visiting the abbey inquire for the cemetery, passing which take the first lane to the left, through a gate, and just before reaching another gate is the stile and footpath. Following this till a road is reached, turn a few yards to the left, and then the road to the top of High Beech is on the right. The return journey may be made by road, but I need not waste time in indicating it, because I am confident that whoever explores this footpath will desire to return by the way that he came.

The Abbey Church of Waltham is one of the very few edifices of importance that date from before the Norman Conquest. Putting aside mere blocks of broken wall, as at Richborough, Tintagel, and Old Sarum, and the ancient church at Canterbury, parts of which were constructed when the Romans ruled this island, and a few small churches in remote hamlets more or less of Saxon origin, it would be difficult to find anything more ancient than Waltham. The nave alone is now standing; and according to the accepted tradition the body of Harold, the last of the Saxons, lies about forty yards eastward of the eastern end of the church as it is now. The tomb bore the inscription in Latin, "Here lies Harold the Unfortunate." If the final resting-place of the valiant warrior of Sendac be only a matter of probability, there can be no doubt that Harold himself was the builder of the church. The architects, however, were Norman, and the nave, though much smaller, bears a striking resemblance to that of Durham. The painted wooden roof—after the style of Peterborough —the eastern windows, and the reredos, are quite modern restorations. The heavy ivy-mantled tower at the westward end was built out of the stones of the dismantled portion in the time of Queen Mary. On this tower is indicated where the keys are kept, and no visitor to Waltham should be satisfied without a peep at the interior. Immediately to the left of the tower is a pathway leading to the old abbey gate, bearing the arms of Edward III., and if the rambler follows the mill stream a few yards further he will come to a small ancient bridge which bears the name of Harold. Waltham is connected by tradition with a yet earlier Saxon King, for the numerous channels of the Lea in the neighbourhood are said to owe their origin to the work of Alfred in diverting the course of the river so as to leave the Danish ships aground.

For an alternative route we will start from Chingford Station, and make directly for the New Hotel and Queen Elizabeth's Lodge, the latter, which has lately been renovated, being a house of considerable age, though of no great architectural pretensions. On the way from the station to the hotel the rambler cannot but be struck with the great stretch of open ground, forest land but without a tree, the furrows plainly visible. For many a year to

come it will remain thus—a silent, but eloquent, witness of
the greed of land-grabbers and the folly of the Woods and
Forests Office.   This is the stolen land that has been restored to the people.   The view of the forest country across
Fairmead Plain northward to High Beech is charming, but
we press forward and find in front of the hotel an orna-
mental piece of water, at the far end of which is a path,
only passable in dry weather, leading us in the direction of
the square water tower at Buckhurst Hill.   On coming
near the hill make for the church, where there is a picturesque landscape, embracing the high ground on the other
side of the Roding Valley.   Turning back down the lane
by the side of the church we are soon in the Epping Road
once more.   Let us follow this road—of course I simply
mean keep it in sight—for a mile or two, till we reach the
Robin Hood.   Nearly half-a-mile beyond is a broad track
on the right leading towards Loughton.   Some little distance to the right is a thicket, and inside the thicket, if
you can only find the way to penetrate it, is an ancient
British camp, the site much obscured by the trees, but
commanding extensive views.   I must leave the rambler
to find it if he can, for I cannot put on paper directions
when all the landmarks are trees of about equal height.
Unless my companion has plenty of time to spare I would
advise him not to try it, especially as when he reaches the
point at which he would turn from the main road he will
see a path to the left instead of to the right, leading him
over high ground that commands substantially the same
prospect, not only of Essex, but of the distant Kentish hills
between Gravesend and Woolwich.   The path leads up to
the King's Oak, the scenery about which I have already
described.   Let the rambler then inquire for Fairmead
Lodge, soon after passing which he will find a broad green
opening to the right, which he will follow for some little
distance; but when he finds the track bending to the left,
he should leave it, and strike straight across the open
ground westward till he reaches a lane leading up Leppitt's
Hill.   At the top of the hill, opposite the Owl, there is a
stile, and in the second field there is a view right across
London to the Crystal Palace, with Highgate and the
towers of the Alexandra Palace in mid-distance.   Thence
we turn back to the end of the lane, and easily find our

way turning sharp off to the right, till we reach our original starting point at Chingford Station. The whole round is not more than eight miles, and including, as it does, Buckhurst Hill, High Beech, and Leppitt's Hill, it embraces the chief points of vantage from which to view the surrounding country.

WINCHMORE HILL.

TWENTY years ago the North Londoner found himself out in the clear as soon as he had traversed the road which the builders called Highbury New Park. The Sluice House and Hornsey Wood House were the only buildings that he passed in walking from Highbury New Park, up Cut-throat Lane, over the hill into Hornsey. We must go much further a-field now to get clear of the bricks and mortar. Even Hornsey and Wood Green have grown into populous suburbs; in that direction we must go as far as Winchmore Hill before we can be rid of the signs of proximity to the Metropolis. I remember the time when the wants of Winchmore Hill, as regards locomotion, were supplied by one small omnibus daily; now it may be reached from either Broad Street (N.L.R.) or Moorgate Street (G.N.R.) or intermediate stations for rather less than 1s. 4d. return. The time is approaching when it will share the fate of Hornsey and Wood Green; but as yet the builders have only made occasional raids upon it, and its beauty is still unimpaired. It is not a parish, and has no ancient buildings; though it is worthy of note that Thomas Hood once lived here, at Rose Cottage, Vicar's Moor Lane, which has been appropriately re-christened "Hood's Own." On leaving the station the first feeling is one of disappointment. You can hardly realise that you are on a hill at all. Thangbrand Olaf's priest told the Icelanders that three women and one goose made a market in their town; so a respectable heap of gravel makes a hill in north-eastern Middlesex. Small as it is, however, Winchmore Hill is by no means to be despised. At least, it is rich in sylvan wealth; no matter which direction you take, the roads and lanes are delightfully shaded. Here, as everywhere else, taverns are so obtrusive that they need no mention; but if the humble pedestrian wants a cup of tea and other re-

B

freshments he can obtain it close to the station at one of
the houses in the short lane leading to Gray's Wood.

This suburban railway station is but three minutes'
walk of a delightful wood. You have but to turn to the
right on leaving it and keep straight forward, keeping the
pond on your right, and you pass straight into the path.
It has a somewhat thin appearance, since the lower branches
of the trees are lopped, but below it is thick fern brake, and
the view around is truly rural. When at length the
rambler emerges into a road he may turn a little to the
right, and, taking the first lane to the left, he will soon find
on his right once more a footpath across open meadows,
which will afford him charming views of the surrounding
country, including the Alexandra Palace to the south, and
the Essex Hills to the east. He is upon high ground all
the way, till at last he reaches an open green at Southgate.
Here let him turn to the left, the road having a wide
margin of green turf, with a fringe of lofty elms. As he
descends, when he finds the main road bends to the left,
let him keep straight forward. There are charming views
along this winding lane; even the pond and the ancient
high red-brick wall, and the gateway at the far end of it,
will not fail to please the rambler who has an eye for the
picturesque. At last he will strike across a main road into
King's Arms Lane, then, after passing a nursery ground
on both left and right, he will bear to the left, when in
doubt, and take the first field-path on the right, across field
after field, till at last he strikes into a lane, where he will
turn to the right. Opposite a park gate he will find a lane
to the left, and in the distance among the trees he will see
the square tower of Edmonton Church. Proceeding up
this lane a little way, after passing a windmill, he will find
a path to the right that leads him straight to the church;
all the way there are distant views of Muswell and Winchmore and Enfield Hills to the westward, and of High Beech,
Sewardstone, and Chingford to the eastward. Edmonton
Church has an ancient square stone tower; the poverty of
its modern brickwork is hidden by carefully-trained ivy.
The churchyard is the burial-place of Charles Lamb.
Taking the road to the left from the church by Hyde Side,
let us strike into the first footpath to the left across the
meadows, which affords us in front pleasant prospects of

the wooded slopes of Winchmore Hill, and, behind, distant prospects of the Essex Hills. Reaching a high road, and crossing it, we press straight forward up a lane (Ford's Grove), under the grateful shade of arching oaks and elms, till once more we reach the railway station, the whole circuit being somewhat less than six miles.

Now for a second route, which the ardent rambler may easily add to the first. Turning to the right on leaving the station, let us strike off sharp to the right on reaching the green. In a few minutes we shall reach a turning to the right called Vicar's Moor Lane. Some little distance down this lane is a footpath to the left, that soon affords us a delightful view to the northward, which comes upon us with a pleasant surprise, and which we reluctantly turn from, when once more we emerge into a road, though the rambler may, if he pleases, keep the path straight forward along the path opposite him, hereafter described. Turning to the right we find that the road leads us into the high road to Enfield, but that road as we turn to the left up the hill leads us under a canopy of arching trees. At the top of the hill we find a footpath straight before us which commands splendid views of the Essex Hills on the right. At last we strike again into the Enfield Road, and turning to the right we keep straight forward till Enfield itself is reached, when we turn to the left through the broad highway. Passing Chase Green on the right, we ascend the hill, and if we are tired the G.N.R. station is handy for the return journey. Otherwise, let us go on to the crown of the hill, which is a commanding eminence, though not lofty. Descending the hill some little distance, just beyond a new house with a red porch, we shall find to the left a footpath leading across the meadows for some distance along the valley, with smiling uplands on either hand. The path leads into a narrow green lane, which ascends the slope, one of the prettiest and most secluded portions of our ramble. When at length we reach our starting point at Winchmore Hill, we shall find the circuit to have been rather less than five miles.

I know that many pedestrians object to be treated as capital offenders of old, who were sentenced to be taken to the place from whence they came. They prefer to go right on. The long-distance walker may take Edmonton as a starting point, and foot it to Winchmore Hill, as above indicated. We will join him at the station, and take the footpath northwards in Vicar's Moor Lane. When we come out into a road we see straight before us a range of wooded hills, and an opening leading towards them through a market garden. Let us follow this track up the hill, stopping at the summit to admire the surrounding slopes. A little further we strike into a road, but we find almost opposite us a footpath, descending along which we at length reach the New River. The banks on both sides are skirted with trees, and for more than half-a-mile we have a delightful combination of wood and water. No visitor to either Winchmore Hill or Enfield should miss this charming spot. I am almost tempted to ask the printer to put this sentence in capitals.

On leaving the river path we find ourselves at Chase Green, Enfield. We turn to the left up the hill, past the G.N.R. Station. Just beyond the house with a red porch is the dry-weather path, above described, back to Winchmore Hill, but we push forward along the road for two or three miles. If it happens to be dusty, let me plead in excuse for it that it not only commands pleasant views, but is for a considerable distance green bordered, and for the most part well shaded in the afternoon. At the end we turn to the right; the green slopes of Enfield are in mid distance, and the long range of Essex Hills beyond. Just beyond the white lodges of Brent Park, we shall find a turning to the left leading to the Cock Inn. A few yards before reaching the Inn is a narrow turning to the right, which, as it has a gate across it a little way down, the rambler would take for a private road. As soon as he passes through the gate he will no longer wonder why I have brought him here. We are now at Hadley Common, the most uncommon Common that ever you did see. It, at least, deserves to be called a wood; and if it were much larger than two hundred acres it would deserve to be dignified as a forest. It is on the slopes of two hills. At first it is but a narrow slip, a noble stretch of park land on one side, New Barnet and High Barnet on the other. Once across the dip, the Common broadens, and as we ascend we find ourselves in one of the noblest pieces of woodland to be found in the Northern suburbs. The sylvan beauty of this sequestered spot is almost unrivalled. If newspapers were printed in the style adopted by Parliamentary Whips, I should score at least half a dozen lines under this last sentence. No North Londoner should miss an early opportunity of becoming acquainted with this delightful spot.

Emerging at length from the woods, we reach a broad green open space, on the opposite side of which is the pretty rural church of Hadley. Passing through the churchyard, we reach the green, and, keeping the main road on the right, we soon reach another green, from the further end of which we take a peep at the Hertfordshire Hills. Turning about a hundred yards to the right along the main road, we reach a small obelisk which records the fact that here, or hereabouts, was fought the great battle of Barnet, in which Warwick the King-maker was slain by the soldiers of Edward IV. Turning back, we follow the road into High Barnet, G.N.R. (fare 9d.).

Note that just above High Barnet Station is a charming footpath to the right that leads across the main line to the far end of Hadley Common, which return excursionists to Hadley *via* Barnet should take, returning as above described through the Common and Hadley.

HAMPSTEAD.

WHAT! Hampstead Heath? Donkey rides, steam roundabouts, swings, boiling water 2d., tea and water-cress 9d., *al fresco* under the willows of the Vale of Health? Well, if this is all that is remembered of Hampstead, let me urge my readers to pay it just one more visit, paying special attention to its odd nooks and corners. Moreover, to many South Londoners the inner northern suburbs are almost unknown, and equally so are the southern suburbs to the northern residents. Those of us who spent our youth in Central London, but have been scattered by the irresistible centrifugal force, meet one another now and then in the middle of the day, either in the City or the West-end; but, for the most part, our families are as widely separated as though they lived fifty miles apart. We mostly keep to our own railway lines and our own side of the water. I have often noticed that through trains of the G.N.R.,

Midland, and L.C.&D.R. Companies are never so empty as between Farringdon Street and Snow Hill. Primarily, though not exclusively, this article is for South Londoners.

I spoke of Hampstead nooks and corners; let me emphasize this expression. Every middle-aged Cockney knows that the old houses of Central London are rapidly disappearing. Cheapside, Cannon Street, Leadenhall Street, Holborn, are very different from what they used to be when we were boys together. We still find the old suburban villas scattered about amid long lines of modern bricks and mortar at Clapton, Tottenham, Streatham, Clapham, Stockwell, Hackney, and Kensington, but there is only one suburban locality in which the eighteenth century still predominates, and that is Hampstead. I grant that the domestic architecture of the Tudor period is infinitely more picturesque, and I concede that the houses of the last century are somewhat tame and formal; but the domestic architecture of our great-great-grandfathers, now that it is mellowed by time, is by no means to be despised, and if it be true that imitation is the sincerest flattery, then old Hampstead needs no further vindication at my hands.

In the Finchley Road are three railway stations—Metropolitan (Swiss Cottage), Midland, and North London—either of which will serve as a convenient starting point. A few yards after passing the third, on the right, is a footpath up a hillside meadow, which commands an extensive view over western London, with the Surrey Hills as a back ground. On striking into a lane we turn to the right, afterwards to the left. Following this lane to the top, then swerving a little to the left, and up some steps on the right, we shall reach a secluded corner of the heath, which comes upon us with a sudden burst of beauty. But I would rather advise the rambler to keep on moving, up and down and in and out, at his own sweet will, keeping his eyes open all the while. Almost every house and wall is an old-world picture, pleasant to the eye, if boasting of nothing more than thick casements bordered with red brick, pleasanter still if half hid in roses and jessamine, with windows in the gabled roofs. I have no great love for pollarded trees, but here they are so strictly in keeping with eighteenth century trimness that they but add to the beauty of the scene. Halfway up the lane (Frognal) is a walk leading to Mount Vernon; some little distance along this walk is a lane to the right, leading down to the churchyard, from which we can obtain an extensive view over London. Retracing our steps, and pursuing our way a little further, we command a still more extensive prospect; but, whichever way we turn, we are surrounded by ancient mansions and cottages, with bright glimpses over London southward. On the other side of the main road, about Christ Church and Well Walk, are pleasant umbrageous ways, though here the presence of modern London is somewhat unpleasantly obtrusive. Because I know that not one person in ten who is familiar with the heath is acquainted with the village, I emphatically underscore it.

The grand view northward and westward from the main road across the heath is too well known to need much lengthened description. Always beautiful, it is seen best towards sunset, when the noble sheet of water in the middle distance seems like a sea of glass mingled with fire. Let me recommend those who are already familiar with the scene to strike off to the left, when they stand by the flagstaff near Jack Straw's Castle, till they reach a road with a fence beyond. Crossing the fence into a walk with a strip of green sward, they will find, somewhat lower down the hill, a stile that leads to another eminence. From the top of this last, close by a cluster of cottages, is the most extensive view in the neighbourhood, commanding not only a wide sweep northward, but a splendid view of London to the south, with the Surrey Hills beyond. On returning, let the rambler skirt the northernmost limits of the heath, which are delightfully shaded, till he climbs up to the cluster of tall cedars at the extreme end of the high road, close to the Spaniards Inn. Passing by the Spaniards Inn, along Hampstead Lane, he may have a choice of roads. The first lane on the left is soon contracted into a mere footpath across pleasant meadows, that lead up the gentle slope of East End, Finchley. On striking into a high road opposite, but a few yards to the right is a path through a gate, leading across the railway into a lane, which, if followed to the right, leads by another footpath to East End Station. Here the rambler may inquire his way to Muswell Hill, and follow the undulating and green-bordered road to Hornsey.

The alternative route from Hampstead Lane is a little further on. There is a short lane on the right, which apparently leads nowhere, but at the end the rambler will find a footpath, enclosed by high fences, but skirting Caen Wood, whose arching trees furnish a grateful shade. The few who know this charming suburban footway will excuse me for pausing to recommend it to the many who do not. The footpath, after a time, becomes a lane, and the lane grows into a high road, which leads at length into the Highgate Road near the "Duke of St. Albans," which inn lies a little to the right, where omnibuses stand ready to carry the rambler back to the West-end of London. If the rambler wishes to return to town by way of the City, he will take the lane by the side of the "Duke of St. Albans," passing between Highgate Cemetery and the delightful group of houses which Baroness Burdett-Coutts has called Holly Village, the latter well worth a visit. From this point he can easily inquire his way to the Archway Tavern, where there are trams which will take him back to the City for 3d.

I must not omit notice of another footpath, even though it be very familiar to North Londoners. On the southern side of the heath, in a straight line from Well Walk, is a path that leads through brickfields, across pleasant undulating meadows. To the right is the ever-extending Metropolis, to the left the dark foliage of Caen Wood, in front the steep of Highgate, with the church crowning the hill. Crossing a lane we find the footpath grows into a lane which leads to the upper part of the Highgate Road, when we turn up the hill. At more than one opening southward it is well worth while to turn a few yards to glance over distant London, though to pursue these lanes far is sheer waste of time. On reaching the main road from Holloway, we may pass forward through Southwood Lane to Highgate Station, or, turning towards London down the hill, turn to the left into Hornsey Lane, across the Archway—a fine piece of engineering work—which commands a fine view of the northern suburbs. Thence we pass by trim suburban villas to Crouch End Station, just before passing which, to the left, is a footway leading across the line, which will take us to high ground, commanding an extensive prospect of the Essex hills, and from which there is more than one way down to Finsbury Park.

I would suggest to those who are already well acquainted with the Hampstead district the next time they take a stroll that way to take the poems of John Keats with them. The name of Keats is inseparably associated with Hampstead, and to me it has always seemed that his poetry is almost as much saturated with its quiet beauty as that of Wordsworth is with the Lake district. The century has grown old since Adonais walked these ways, yet still, on the open heath, "the prickly furze buds lavish gold"; in the lane leading to Highgate there is still "a scent of blossoming limes"; around Child's Hill "the willow trails its delicate amber"; in the open fields between the heath and Highgate, at spring-time, "the daisies, vermeil-rimmed and white, hide in deep herbage," and in summer they are sweet with the smell of "comfortable green and juicy hay." Everywhere there are "cool and bunchéd leaves" above: "trees old and young sprouting a shady boon for simple sheep"; below "the quaint mossiness of aged roots." Vast as is the growth of London, we may still find here "some melodious spot of beechen green," which is "the murmurous haunt of flies on summer eves"; we may still wander "through verdurous glooms and mossy winding ways"; and, though within sight of the great city when we are on the heights, descending to the hollows, "in the bosom of a leafy world we rest in silence." To you, as to me, let Nature speak as she spoke more than half-a-century ago to the surgeon's apprentice, and in the sweet singer she has a noble interpreter.

EPSOM.

THE vast majority of the visitors to Epsom Downs know as little of the surrounding country as of racehorses. When the equestrians have left, leaving behind them any quantity of greasy paper, broken bottles, and other litter, defiling the fair face of Nature, we modest pedestrians will pay a visit to the little Surrey town whose mineral springs made it a fashionable watering place two centuries

ago. Of course the obvious way by road is through
Tooting, Mitcham, and Sutton; which, though quite good
enough for Derby-day people, is about as tame and uninteresting a country road as I ever travelled. The obvious
way by rail is to Epsom, S.W.R., or Epsom Downs,
L.B.S.C.R. (single 1s. 2d., return 2s. 2d.); or the rambler
who wants a moderate walk can leave the train at Sutton,
when he will soon find himself on Banstead Downs, and
pursue his way forward till he reaches the Epsom Downs
Station. The view is too well known to need description;
but I must admit that, though very extensive, it is somewhat disappointing. Line beyond line, each growing
fainter, it gives the idea of immense distance, at some
points looking like a remote sea; but the radical defect is
that the foreground takes up three-fourths of the picture.
It is not Epsom Downs, but the surrounding country that
attracts me to the spot.

We pedestrians are not as other men, and the obvious
ways are just those which we naturally avoid. To reach
Epsom let us take a ticket at Waterloo for Surbiton (1s.).
We enquire for the Leatherhead Road, and follow it for a
couple of miles. Though here and there it presents
pleasing views of the surrounding country, by the time we
reach Hook my companion will be ready to ask whether
he needed a guide for this sort of thing. A little more
patience, my friend! Just past Lower Hook Gate, a side
bar which we go by, not go through, there is an inn, and
a little beyond it on the left a footpath, through the fields,
with gentle upland scenery on either hand, which brings
us to the little rustic church of Chessington. Now and
again on our way we have caught occasional glimpses of
the Downs; but here they are full in sight, and the
distance lends enchantment to the view. It is a truly
glorious panorama. To the left, towards Cheam and
Sutton, the valley is so thickly wooded that it looks like a
great forest. Before us, and stretching away far to the
right to the back of Box Hill, is the long ridge of hills,
and in the middle distance a gentle pastoral country of
most inviting beauty, through which we have to pass.
The footpath is before us, directly opposite the churchyard. At the end of the first field the prospect to the
left grows more extensive, and includes Kingston Hill and

Wimbledon, and far in the distance the towers of Sydenham. At the beginning of the next field we take the left-hand path, and as we descend we turn to survey the umbrageous uplands which we have just left. In a field further on, where the path may seem doubtful, we pass through the gate at the extreme corner, and in the next field keep a sharp look out for a stile on the left. Crossing this we soon emerge into a lane, when, a yard or two on the right, we shall find another footpath that brings us by a straight course into Epsom. The distance is not much more than five miles. In spite of its uninteresting commencement, I would recommend it with all the emphasis at my command.

Let us now take another route, which a good pedestrian, who does not mind adding seven or eight miles to the five just described may combine with that already indicated. We will start from Epsom Station, and proceed up the well-known road to the Grand Stand. Proceeding almost in a straight line we cross the racecourse, just cutting off Tattenham Corner, and, crossing the course again, strike into a lane, when we turn to the right, where we shall find a bright prospect of the woods to the south, with Walton Church in the centre. The lane itself skirts a pleasant wood, where we may rest awhile, and pursue our way through it for a time, keeping close to the road. By and bye we reach cross-roads, but striking straight forward the lane soon becomes a mere footpath that leads us upon a wide common, thick with broom and heather and fern-brake, with the tower of Kingston Church as a landmark. At the church we strike into the Reigate Road, and following it to the right we find it pleasantly shaded from the afternoon side, alternately by wide-arching trees, and high banks, thickly planted with fragrant hawthorns. After passing "The Fox" we look out for a sign-post directing us down a lane on the left to Upper Gatton. We follow this lane till we reach four cross-roads, when we turn to the left, and a few yards on the right is a stile and a footpath so little trodden that it might be easily mistaken. Follow this through one or two fields, and then, as it begins to descend from the high ground, you will come upon a landscape that, once seen, will never be effaced from memory. To the left is the range of chalk

hills extending eastward from Merstham; to the right
another ridge on which stand Nutfield and Bletchingley;
in the rich valley between Godstone lies half hidden amid
the trees, and in the far distance are the Kentish Hills
towards Tunbridge Wells; while as we descend we catch
occasional glimpses behind us and to the extreme right of
the thick woods of Gatton Park, the heights around Red
Hill, and the Weald of Sussex beyond. The traveller
who is whisked past Merstham Station, on his way to
Brighton or Hastings, can form no idea of the wealth of
beauty around him. Where the footpath breaks into the
roadway we follow the road to the left for a short distance,
when we shall find another stile to the right, leading us
over undulating ground with pleasant, if more contracted,
views, and descending again, across rich pastures, we find
ourselves at last in the village of Merstham. Turning to
the left, past quaint ancient cottages, we reach the ivy-
covered gates and ivy-covered lodge leading to Lord
Hylton's mansion, just to the right of which is a swing
gate, through which we pass along a path adorned by
wood and water leading us to Merstham Church, situated
in a delightful leafy nook. Then retracing our steps, we
soon come to Merstham (S.E.R.), where a fare of 1s. 6d.
will bring us back once more to the great city.

Yet another route through the pleasant Epsom district.
We will start for Caterham Junction, S.E.R. and L.B.S.C.R.
(fare 1s. 1d.), and turning into the main road follow it to
the left till we reach the Red Lion, just after passing
which we bear to the right. On the way we cannot fail
to have noticed a footpath up a hill straight before us; we
shall soon find the way to it behind a chalk mound. It is a
deviation, but we have come out to see the country, not
to find short cuts. At the top of the hill the prospect is
grand, extending straight before us down the valley to
Croydon, embracing the heights around it, while far
away in the distance a blaze of light marks the Sydenham
Palace. At the summit of the hill is thick copse, one of
those quiet resting places that remind us of Longfellow's
lines—

"Where the dark foliage interweaves
In one unbroken roof of leaves,
Underneath whose sloping eaves

Just beyond the copse is a charming landscape south-ward. Retracing our steps through the copse, we shall find straight before us a path leading down the hill, which we follow till we reach a road, when, turning to the left, we proceed till we reach a lane with a signpost indicating Banstead. It soon forks, the lower way leading to Banstead Station. We take the upper, which commands the verdant-looking hills opposite; and as we toil upwards through the open down we, of course, take the elastic turf. At the top of the hill a lane shaded with noble elms, and affording a peep now and then of the heights to the east, brings us to Banstead, just after entering which a meadow path to the left brings us to the pretty church. Leaving the churchyard on the northern side, we may, if tired of our six-mile ramble, turn to the left to Banstead Station, on the Downs, where the view is substantially the same as that from the racecourse. Otherwise we turn to the right for a four-mile walk to Carshalton. The signposts in-dicate the lane, which is for the most part bordered by towering hedges or shaded by lofty trees. Some distance forward on the left is "The Oaks," one of the noblest pieces of sylvan scenery in Surrey. We skirt this on two sides, and can enjoy it almost as much from outside as inside. Thence to Carshalton the road invites no further comment. Carshalton itself is a place where anyone could spend an agreeable half-holiday. From the surrounding parks half-a-dozen clear streams meet in the centre of the village, forming the head-waters of the Wandle. All its surroundings are bright and attractive, and the wayfarer can easily obtain directions how to proceed by charming bye-ways to Beddington and other neighbouring villages. We, however, will make for the station, just before enter-ing which we find a village workman's club, where we obtain refreshments at moderate prices. With its carpeted rooms, its well-stored library, its billiard and bagatelle tables, and its pianos, this may be pronounced the most comfortable and well-appointed place of the kind in any of our smaller suburban villages.

so level that, save for the keen breezes that blow across it, and for occasional glimpses of distant heights, you would not suspect that you are on a hill at all. We keep straight forward across the turf; there is hardly enough traffic to make a cart track, but we can see Caterham straight before us. At the end of the common we follow the road into Caterham, and the finger-posts take care that we shall not miss White Hill.

Soon after passing the Water Works we find on the right a view commanding all Northern Surrey, with the faint blue line of the Middlesex Hills in the far distance beyond. It comes upon us with a pleasant sense of surprise, for ever since reaching Kenley Common the road has been so level that we have lost our recollection of the hill we climbed after passing Kenley Station; but there are richer beauties yet in store for us. As soon as we reach a low square tower a little distance from the road on the left we shall find on the right an open gate and a footpath. The prospect before us is magnificent. Looking from the steep brow of White Hill the eye takes in a wide range of country, bounded only by the high ridge of Sussex Downs that rise between us and the sea; it is said, indeed, that at one point, on a clear day, the ships are visible from the tower itself. Be that as it may, on the left we have the wooded slopes of Gatton Park, and the yet loftier woods at the back of Reigate Hill; beyond, to the south-west, the long ascent of Leith Hill jutting boldly out on the lowlands, its tower rising in the distance no higher than a mere milestone; due south is the far distant line of the South Downs, and eastward ridge after ridge of the pleasant Kentish Hills. Yet to my thought the most charming feature of this glorious landscape is the view in the middle distance. Beyond the rich valley immediately at our feet, where again and again it has been my good fortune in the pleasant spring-time to walk ankle deep in English grass, there is a gentle verdant ridge of hills, whose comparative lowliness only enhances its beauty, since it does not shut out the distant country beyond. The fainter lines and softer colours seen far across the Weald of Sussex only set off the luscious verdure of this intervening slope. Half hidden among the trees are Tandridge, Godstone, Bletchingley, and Nutfield, and a little further to the right is Red Hill, with Earlswood just beyond it. There are heights around London which have a far more popular reputation, and each of them well deserves the fame which it has achieved. I am familiar with them all. High Beech, Hendon, Harrow, Winchmore, Stanmore, Weybridge, Banstead, Shirley, Keston, Chislehurst, Shooter's Hill, and Box Hill have each beauties of their own, which I willingly acknowledge; but most of them are inferior to, and not one of them surpasses, the grand panorama of White Hill.

When the rambler is sufficiently satiated with the glorious beauties around him, he may, if tired, return by the road he came to Caterham Station, otherwise he would do well to follow the footpath. At the end of the first field he will find that it strikes into another, which gives him the choice upward or downward. He may, if he pleases, turn upward, seeing that it gives him a somewhat higher vantage ground for surveying the surrounding country; but he will find, if he pursues it to the end, that it only leads to farm buildings, and he will consequently have to return to the point from which he started. But if he has not taken a return-ticket to Caterham let him turn downwards instead of upwards; Merstham Station (S.E.R., single 1s. 6½d.) is only two or three miles distant, and all the way he will have around him the scenery of which I have just spoken. The path at length turns into a lane, and the only direction he has to observe is that just after passing two brick pillars supporting heraldic figures, he turns to the left and takes a path across the fields a few yards on the right. If he finds himself under the necessity of waiting for a train, the entrance to Lord Hylton's park and Merstham Church are well worth a visit.

As an alternative route for those who wish to see a little of the hill country on either side of the valley, let me suggest the following:—On the eastern side of the valley along Riddlesdown there are plenty of obvious footpaths, though, as I said before, I give the preference to the one opposite the "Rose and Crown." On returning into the road make for Kenley Station, a short distance towards London. Cross the railway bridge, and keep straight up the lane immediately facing you. It is one of those narrow, green, shady lanes for which Surrey is so famous. When nearly at the top of the hill it bends, and soon you will find, on looking back, a break between the hills, with Croydon in mid-distance and the Norwood heights beyond. Proceed till a swing gate is reached on the right, turning through which we shall soon find ourselves descending into another narrow little valley with a thickly wooded hill opposite. We shall find another footpath leading up this hill through the wood, and, at the top, level green sward, with the odd little rustic church of Coulsdon on the left. Just after passing this we take the road to the left, which brings us to Coulsdon Common, a broad level tract, richly covered with purple heather. After crossing this we shall find the road forks; we take the left hand one, and follow it till we reach an open green, where we shall find a footpath skirting it on the left. At the end of this is a narrow green lane straight before us, by which we gradually descend into the Caterham Valley again. The sylvan beauty of this walk would alone make it a very attractive one, but the prospect before us is truly delectable. The opposite hills are far superior to Riddlesdown, being well wooded, loftier, and more undulating. Once again in the road the rambler may turn up the lane opposite to Warlingham, or along the road to the right till he reaches Caterham Station.

GRAVESEND.

OWING to steamboat competition, the South-Eastern Railway issues return tickets to Gravesend for 1s. 6d., available by certain trains only. It is the cheapest railway ride for its length that I know—rather too long, perhaps, considering the comfortless character of most South-Eastern Railway third-class carriages. If the wives and daughters of the directors would travel up and down the line every day for a week, getting in and out at a few intermediate stations, I would willingly trust them as a jury to acquit me of a libel when I brand these vehicles as narrow to the point of downright indecency. As the South-Eastern Railway, however, offers us the cheapest railway ride out of London we will gladly avail ourselves of it.

The town itself need not detain us long; familiarity breeds contempt. It possesses some architectural monstrosities that are almost inimitable in their ugliness, innumerable shrimp shops, and two piers. Our grandfathers used to stay there as we stay at Brighton or Margate. Well do I remember my first acquaintance with the place, just after a great fire which had laid half the narrow main street in ashes. It is not greatly altered now. You may still ascend Windmill Hill at the back of the town, from whence there is a commanding view of the river and the surrounding country; Rosherville Gardens still invite you to spend a happy day, where you can dance "every day and all day long" if so disposed; and you can still walk along the river side to the furthermost tavern, "The Ship and Lobster." For such attractions as these the holiday excursionist needs no guide; but the rambler who cares not for the madding crowd, and to whom the marsh and mud of a tidal river suggest that distance lends enchantment to the view, will regard Gravesend simply as a starting point for fresh fields and pastures new. We visit Gravesend only at once to get away from it.

Leaving Gravesend Station we turn up Windmill Street; when the very last house is reached straight before us is a lane and a footpath. Of course we take the latter. The open fields are not very picturesque, but they command extensive views of the surrounding country. The path brings us to the hamlet of Singlewell, when we turn down the road to the left, but at the first stile once more to the right, across the fields and hop gardens. A second time we reach a lane, but turning to the left again, a few yards further we find another footpath, leading across the fields in the direction of the wooded hills which have been full in sight during the greater part of the walk. Keeping the main track when we find diverging paths, we shall presently strike into a lane which bends a little away from the hills, and once more a field-path brings us to the village of Cobham. Opposite the "Leather Bottle," which has been immortalised in Dickens's *Pickwick Papers*, is the church, behind which are interesting fabrics of an ancient chantry. Hard by is a college for twenty pensioners, built in the time of Elizabeth. Returning into the street we proceed till we reach the cross-roads, where the view to the south is very charming, while on the left is a gate through which we can admire a noble avenue of grand old elms that leads up to Cobham Hall. On Fridays the house is shown to visitors who have previously obtained tickets at Caddell's, booksellers, at Gravesend or Rochester. We take the Rochester Road and soon find a stile leading into the park. The path leads towards a drive, and passing through a gate we reach the woods, which are magnificent. The last time I was there, finding no barriers, I wandered about among the mossy ways, as soft as velvet, admiring the beauty of Lord Darnley's trees, until a person of the gamekeeping persuasion politely invited me to go back. I apprehend that any other gentle pilgrim in search of the beautiful will meet with no worse fate. But timid souls who fear to tread on a noble lord's daisies need not be deterred, for the road back towards Gravesend proceeds for some distance through the woods—arching branches above, thick fern brake below—and will well repay them for the walk. These woodlands, even if you only keep to the road, are unsurpassed in their wild secluded beauty. Just after reaching a cluster of red-brick cottages, whose exterior, at least, says much for Lord Darnley's taste and benevolence, a footpath on the left through cornfields leads us back straight to Gravesend. The whole circuit is not more than eight or nine miles.

So deeply am I impressed with the enchanting beauty of the Cobham Woods that I must here indicate the way to reach them without taking in Cobham itself, thus shortening the ramble by three miles. Let the rambler follow Parrock Street, Gravesend, and the road beyond it till the last house is passed, follow the lane till it becomes a path, and make straight towards the wooded heights. He will find lanes and paths leading to the right, but, avoiding them, he should keep straight on by cart track or path till he reaches a high road, when he has only to turn to the right and he will reach the desired spot. Of course the former route indicated is preferable, being much more comprehensive. Lovers of natural beauty who have never yet seen Cobham would certainly do well to take an early opportunity of making its acquaintance.

Gravesend may also be taken as a convenient starting point for Rochester. The distance by road is only seven miles, and the return journey by rail will only bring up the total cost of the excursion from 1s. 6d. to 2s. 1d. The Rochester Road affords views of the shining reaches of the river, and rather more than half-way it crosses the far-famed Gad's Hill, where, opposite the " Sir John Falstaff," is the former residence of Charles Dickens. Thence between high sloping banks, covered with verdure, it descends into Stroud, the City of Rochester being just across the bridge.

Old as the White Tower of London is, it has been so modernised as to its exterior, and so surrounded by other buildings, that it gives us but a faint idea of what a Norman castle keep was like. In the noble ruins of Rochester Castle we have one of the finest examples in the country. There are considerable fragments of the outer works still standing; the lofty keep, though roofless, is almost entire, and its upper storeys command a wide view of the Medway, and of the grand amphitheatre of hills round the city. Hard by is the cathedral, which, small though it be, has many points of interest—chiefly its noble western gateway, the crypt, and the rich Norman work in the nave. A little distance south of the cathedral is an open space, on one side of which is a large old red-brick mansion, bearing the name of Restoration House, Charles II. having stayed there a night on his way to London. The narrow main street of Rochester has several buildings of interest, including the hospital for six poor travellers, with which all readers of Dickens are acquainted; the Town Hall, with Sir Cloudesley Shovel's clock; and some fine old half-timbered houses, built, probably, in the fifteenth century. In point of fact, the rambler will find in this small city specimens of the work of every century, from the twelfth to the nineteenth, beginning with the modern bridge and ending with the cathedral crypt, built by Bishop Gundulf, who died in 1108. At the end of the High Street a road on the right takes us up Star Hill, the city recreation ground, from whence there is a fine view in all directions, the rambler having Chatham Dockyard immediately below him and the lines of fortification nearly all round.

Born Cockneys must excuse me for indicating an old familiar way which they knew years ago, but of which

London immigrants, who are numbered by thousands, are probably ignorant. On leaving Gravesend Station, anyone will be able to direct the stranger to the footpath to Springhead. It has the advantage of traversing the fields nearly the whole distance, and of possessing extensive views of the river and of the Essex coast beyond, the Laindon Hills, some miles beyond the Essex shore, being the most prominent heights. After leaving the footpath, a short distance down the road to the right are the Springhead watercress and tea gardens. On Saturdays and Mondays the visitor may possibly find them rather too popular, and the children and babies too numerous; but this leafy nook is pleasantly situated, and family parties find refreshments both cheap and good. Just before reaching Springhead, a path to the left leads straight across the fields to Northfleet, whose gigantic chalkpits are well worth a visit, especially those which have been so long unworked that Nature has had time to cover the surface with tree and shrub, and to adorn the steep sides with innumerable pink blossoms. Visitors to Gravesend for the first time, who prefer to keep along the river bank, should turn westward rather than eastward. With all their great chalk-pits and lime-works, Northfleet and Greenhithe are interesting, and the country at the back towards Swanscombe and Southfleet is delightful; but the banks of the river below Gravesend are too flat and unprofitable for a rambler to waste an hour in traversing them.

WEYBRIDGE AND CHERTSEY.

Hitherto I have confined myself almost exclusively to a 1s. 6d. return fare limit, but there are so many who have no need to grudge an extra shilling or two when in search of the picturesque that it is not desirable to adhere to such a rule too strictly. To the managers of annual outings of City employés who are tired of Box Hill or Virginia Water, or other popular resorts, I would suggest Weybridge or Chertsey. With the river on one side and the woods on the other, what more could be desired? Now and then a Sunday School may find its way so far, but, as a rule, the solitude of these two hills is almost perfect.

On a recent Saturday afternoon, save a small pic-nic party on the summit, I met but one solitary individual during an hour's ramble over St. George's Hills. The two places might be easily included in a day's excursion, even by those who are quickly tired, though I would recommend that the intervening ground should be traversed by railway, as the country is flat, and, though pervaded by sweet rural simplicity, somewhat uninteresting. Both places are reached by the S.W.R.; return fare, Weybridge 2s. 10d., Chertsey 3s. 4d.

Of the quiet little town of Chertsey there is not much to be said. A little way up the main street on the left is a portion of the house of Cowley, the poet, the exterior uninteresting save for its associations. The grand Abbey has long since ceased to be; the bridge is a mile from the station, the river-bank presenting no special attractions. St. Ann's Hill, about a mile from the station, is one of the loveliest spots in one of the loveliest of southern counties. I never waste space on directions where there are houses. or sign-posts; suffice it, therefore, that when the road ascends, just after passing the Golden Grove Inn, we keep up the hill to the right, and we shall soon see on the left-hand side of the road the house of Lady Holland, once the famous residence of Charles James Fox. There are two roads before us; we take the right, and a few yards forward on the left we reach an iron gate leading into the grounds, which, by the courtesy of Lady Holland, are open to the public. If these glorious woodlands were situated down in the valley, they would yet be worthy of their fame; but as it is, though St. Ann's Hill is only two hundred and forty feet high, it can boast not only of sylvan charms, but of commanding views in all directions. At the refreshment cottage there are two openings between the trees; through that on the right the rambler, on a clear day, will recognise the Crystal Palace and the Grand Stand at Epsom, while the other is said to afford to those who have good eyes a distant glimpse of the dome of St. Paul's. Keeping straight forward a little distance we reach another and wider opening, where the heights of Harrow and Highgate are easily recognised; and a little further westward, across the Thames Valley, the faint blue lines of the Buckinghamshire Hills. Straight westward.

the prospect is bounded by the dark wooded heights of
Windsor Forest, and further on there is an extensive view
southward, where between the intervening hills we catch
the distant outlines of the Hog's Back and the chalk downs
between Guildford and Dorking.   There is not one of the
many paths on this hill which does not disclose some fresh
beauty, but whatever else he misses the rambler must be
sure to visit the Anchor Corpse.   Let him go forward
from the refreshment cottage till he reaches a path down
a few wooden steps, and he will soon reach a spot where
six different paths are in view.   Straight before him is a
gate, and beyond a path with a wooded slope on the right
and open country on the left ; it soon turns into a narrow
walk, with an arching canopy of leaves for half-a-mile.
Here I must pause, or the multitudinous beauties of St.
Ann's Hill will leave me no space for Weybridge.

There is no difficulty about the road from Weybridge
Station to St. George's Hills.   On leaving the station, the
rambler takes the road straight forward to the south, and,
after walking about half-a-mile, he will see on the left a
lodge, a gate, and a notice-board.   After entering the gate
let him keep straight forward for a short distance, and
where the path forks take the right-hand road, leading
him to a still pool, in which the surrounding trees are
reflected as in a mirror.   On a still summer day the
silence is profound; save the ants on their myriad-peopled
hills, and an occasional squirrel leaping from bough to
bough, there is no sign of motion.   When the pool is
passed, turn to the left, and he will soon reach the summit
of the hill, where there is a rustic cottage at which light
refreshments may be obtained.   A few yards from this
there is a most extensive view southward, though in other
directions there is only just a peep between the tantalising
trees.   In these extensive woods are numerous walks and
widely varying beauties.   In sultry July weather the
prevalent cold dark green of the Scotch firs is peculiarly
grateful to the eye, and "the solemn minarets of the pine"
which everywhere abound throw into relief the leafy
fountains of the silver birch, and other trees whose
verdancy has yet a brighter shade.   I need hardly say
that the rhododendrons grow thick and luxuriant in the
sandy soil.   For the most part the ground is covered with

impassable fernbrake, relieved here and there with great patches of purple heather. The calm retreat, the silent shade of these sweet woodlands might well content the rambler for half a day, even though he visit them alone. In this restless age we are too much in a hurry even in our holidays. To use an execrable phrase of modern life, we are anxious "to do" scene after scene, just as in the month of May we rush through the crowded rooms of Burlington House, and gain from the whole exhibition far less real pleasure or profit than from the one small *chef d'œuvre* that we can really call our own. Nature, with infinite pity for the weary hand and brain, beckons us to its quiet resting-places, and we get out our maps and guide books, and diligently plan how many of them we can "do" in a day, or a week, or a month, as the case may be. A sea-wave, a tree, or even a piece of moss, will suffice John Ruskin for almost endless delight and contemplation; but we, poor shallow souls such as we are, must needs sprawl ourselves like rivers that have bid adieu to their native mountains across unlimited sands.

So I must take care to satisfy my energetic reader, whose aversion to return tickets is insuperable, and who insists upon going straight on. He shall be satisfied. When on the summit of St. George's Hill let him descend the path before him, bearing on the left when it forks, and to the right when he reaches the main drive. On reaching a sign-post let him turn to the left, and follow that way till it seems to begin to turn up the hill back again. Then he will see a path to the right, which he follows till he comes to a gate leading into a road. Thus far his route has been entirely through woodlands; henceforth to Leatherhead it is mostly by road, but such roads are rare in the neighbourhood of London. The beauty of rivers, like the beauty of woman, depends little upon size; and four times upon our walk we shall come upon the River Mole. We cross it first at the beginning of Cobham. Stand on the bridge looking either way and you have a charming picture. Cross the bridge and take the stile on the right and you will find it yet more attractive. Once again in the road, turn to the left, and the first road on the right leads through Church Cobham, and by the side of the river again for some distance, past a mill, "the dark round of whose dripping wheel" recalls Tennyson's well-known poem. A mile further on the right, just beyond some farm buildings, we can turn into a field-path skirting the road and commanding pleasant prospects of the distant country. Once again in the road we a second time cross the Mole, which from the bridge looks quite as attractive as when we saw it a few miles lower down. Then we mount higher ground, with heather and bracken bushes below, and hollies and oaks above,—by-and-bye skirting tempting woods, with distant glimpses to the south of gentle ascents, which Surrey men know descend into steep declivities towards Dorking and Gomshall. So pleasant is the high road, that we scarcely care to seek any deviating footpath. At a cluster of cottages at the bottom of the hill we are directed to take a lane to the left, which brings us to the Mole once more. We may take the wooden footway if we please, or cool our feet by fording it; the latter, from experience, I would recommend as the more preferable course. The first lane on the right after crossing the river skirts a park on the left, which has a stile in the fence, and here we can see the white winding path up Box Hill and the high ground on the other side of the gap about Denbies and Ranmer Common. At Leatherhead Station, which is now close at hand, we will pause, having traversed rather over a dozen miles, leaving it to more hardy walkers to push on to Box Hill.

DORKING.

FRESH from the sands of Barmouth and mountain grandeur of Cader Idris, I remember byegone years when I had to content myself with lowlier beauty nearer home. The Society journals treat their readers as though the very meanest of them was the younger son of a baronet; and their readers doubtless feel flattered thereby. I, on the contrary, am so rude as to assume that not a few of my readers are troubled by comparative impecuniosity. If sickness, slack trade, unexpected losses have made it difficult to take a holiday at all, and mountain excursions and seaside boarding-houses are out of the question, why not try Surrey? It has twice been my refuge in years gone by; he whom it does not satisfy is hard indeed to please. Open the map, and you will see that a high ridge of chalk downs extends from Godstone to Farnham, right across the county. Along this line the pedestrian will find a continuous panorama of beauty. If time allows, it is best to begin at Sevenoaks, in Kent, and pass by Westerham into Surrey, to Limpsfield Common and Godstone, or else to take train to Caterham (single 1s. 3d.), and walk southward to Godstone, then up the hill beyond, and, taking the road on the right along the ridge, pass by way of Bletchingley and Nutfield to Redhill and Reigate. From the hills north of the latter town the views are magnificent; in preference to that on the main road to Banstead, go through the town and inquire for the footpath leading up the hill to Kingswood. Heedless of the law of trespass, I once kept along the ridge all the way to Box Hill, but I can hardly advise anyone to repeat the experiment. Better return, after enjoying the prospect from the hill, and keep the pleasant valley road to Dorking. Here a diversion should be made to the summit of Leith Hill, of which more hereafter. From Dorking to Guildford the rambler may take his way along the valley through Westcott, Shere, Gomshall, and Albury, climbing to the chapel-crowned height of St. Martha's Hill before reaching Guildford, or he may take the hill road hereinafter indicated.

This guide is designed mainly for day or half-day holiday-makers, but the Surrey tourist may gather hints as to one or two of the most attractive points in his route. Box Hill is so well known that I need hardly dwell upon it, but the visitors to Leith Hill, the highest point in Surrey, are but few. A good pedestrian might climb both in half a day. The nearest station to Box Hill is L.B.S.C.R. (return fare 2s. 10d.). On leaving the station, a short walk brings the rambler into the main road, when, turning a little to the left, he will find the path up Box Hill on his right. From the summit the prospect is magnificent. Leith Hill is about six miles distant. He will have to follow the main road through Dorking till he finds a street to the right (West Street), and follow this till he comes to a sign-post.

directing him to Coldharbour. Twice afterwards, when
in doubt, as there are no sign-posts, he must keep to the
right, along the loveliest of all Surrey lanes. For the
greater part of the distance it passes through woodlands
of surpassing beauty. A third time where the road
forks we turn again to the right, and when we reach
Coldharbour to the right again up the hill, keeping
straight forward along the track till we reach the tower
at the highest point. The prospect from this point is
unequalled in the whole county. Looking southward
over the Weald of Sussex the view is bounded by the
South Downs, and in a gap immediately before us is a
distant glimpse of the English Channel, a little to the
left of Shoreham. Westward, somewhat to the left of
the Hog's Back, is a faint line of high ground, which we
are assured is Salisbury Plain. To the north, beyond
the Surrey Chalk Downs, we can catch a glimpse of the
Crystal Palace, and on a clear day of the dome of St.
Paul's itself. This is truly the half-way house between
London and the sea. The Evelyns of Wootton, to whom
the estate belongs, not only permit the public to wander
about in this delectable country, but have erected a tower
on the highest point, the attendant of which supplies tea
and other refreshments for visitors, and readily affords
information as to the various points of interest. The
rambler would do well to return by a different route,
taking a sheep-track immediately northward from the
tower, which will soon bring him into a green road
between two ranges of hills. Leith Hill is rather a
district than a solitary eminence, and contains within its
bosom wild, secluded valleys, each of which is well
worthy of a visit. The green road brings us at last to a
gate leading into Wootton Park, but, by the grace of
Mr. Evelyn, we go boldly forward to find new and more
cultivated beauties. Soon we come upon an artificial
waterfall upon the right; on the left the water has been
confined in artificial lakes. The trees are worthy of
the inheritor of the name of the author of "Sylva."
Passing out of the park into a lane, we keep straight
forward till we reach the top of the slope, when a path
on the right leads us across the fields and through a
pretty little wood and into another beautiful park,

through another gate, a charming combination of wood and water. Private though it looks, the road is open to the public, and will bring us ere long to the beautiful village of Westcott, whence there is a straight road into Dorking. With a bitter recollection of Dorking inns, I note that of late there has been built in West Street a first-class coffee tavern. Those who are familiar with Box Hill can of course shorten the distance by travelling direct to Dorking; in that case the S.E.R. Station is nearer by nearly a mile than the L.B.S.C.R. Those who start from the S.E.R. Station should turn towards Dorking, and take the first high road to the right till they reach the sign-post indicating the road to Coldharbour. People to whom a 3s. return fare, and nine or ten miles walking is no object, could not do better than take this delightful excursion. At almost every step they will find themselves surrounded by fresh attractions.

But I must not forget my impecunious tourist, who I will presume, after resting for a night at Dorking, wishes to pursue his way westward. If he loves solitude and far-distant prospects, let him look to the hills north by west of the town. Perched up upon the hill is Denbies, the residence of Mr. Cubitt, M.P.; his path lays in that direction. Inquiring the road for the Dorking S.E.R. Station, he passes over the railway bridge, and takes a path to the left across open fields. Emerging into a road, he finds a lane leading up the hill, and just on the left a path that runs parallel with it. He will, of course, take the path, which all the way commands one of the loveliest prospects in Surrey. When he reaches the end, and comes again into the road, he will find himself on Ranmer Common, where he follows the green-bordered road, commanding far-distant views to the north and south. The former is most extensive, as it takes in the whole sweep of country from Weybridge to Sydenham. The Tower of Leith Hill is the most conspicuous object southward, though here and there are distant glimpses of the country beyond. After passing the gate at the end of the common, the rambler should descend the slope till he finds a broad green road facing him, where the gravel road bends. It is so easy to go wrong, and so hard to make the right road clear, that

I hesitate to direct, especially as I once went woefully astray myself; but the charm of this solitary walk—which I believe is part of the old Pilgrim way to Canterbury—is so great that I must make the attempt. After traversing the way for some distance, where a beech-tree marks the divergence of road and footpath, take the road which bends to the left. Follow the track till it merges into a hard road. Follow the hard road nearly half a mile, till it comes to a clump of beeches. There the hard road swerves to the left, but keep straight forward along the green track, and from that point the way is plain. Only let the rambler observe these two directions, and by-and-by he will emerge upon the southern slope of the hills, with St. Martha's Chapel before him on the left, when the wide landscape before him will well repay him for his toil. Just opposite the chapel a finger-post marks the road to Guildford. Disregard the finger-post and keep straight forward along the footpath skirting the cornfields. There is nothing lost in regard to distance, and much gained in point of beauty. At intervals along this charming solitary way are lanes and green walks leading southwards into the valley, each of which is delightful, though it is impossible in the space at my disposal to particularise them. Distance over 19 miles. The villages in the valley between Guildford and Dorking would alone demand a separate paper.

I have noted that all kinds of people anticipating a Bank Holiday complain that every popular place of resort will be crowded. Why not seek places that are not popular? If Box Hill is crowded, the opposite hill is not, and it is equal in all respects. Take a return ticket to Box Hill Station, L.B.S.C.R. (2s. 10d.) On leaving the station turn up the lane over the railway bridge, and follow the road some distance past farm buildings on the right, till you reach a lane to the left uphill. It is worthy of notice that this leads through the most prolific nut-wood in Surrey. At the top is Ranmer Common, with its extensive views in all directions. A little westward of the church is a lane, before described, leading down to Dorking, where the rambler will take care to look out for the footpath, through a swing gate, which runs parallel with the road, and commands delightful scenery. On reaching Dorking the rambler will easily find his way back to the starting point. He may be well content to leave the crowd to the enjoyment of Box Hill, for he has all that they enjoy without the noise and excitement of a popular holiday. The whole circuit is not above six miles, and if that is too much he can shorten the distance by taking a ticket for Box Hill at the Dorking Station of the L.B.S.C.R. There are ramblers who will find it far too short; let them make Leatherhead their starting point (return fare L.B.S.C.R. 2s. 9d.). On leaving the station go through the little town by the street that passes the church. On descending a slope they will find to the right a bridge crossing the Mole by a road that looks private. Just after passing some farm buildings there is a footpath on the left which leads through Norbury Park to the village of Mickleham, on entering which the Mole is again crossed, and yet again at Burford Bridge, where the first turning on the right will lead across the railway close to Box Hill station, and up to Ranmer Common by the route through the nut-wood described above. From an objective point of view a crowd of holiday makers is to me as attractive a spectacle as it was to Goethe's Faust; but subjectively distance lends enchantment to the view. There must be plenty of Bank Holiday makers who are exactly of my mind. For such I would suggest either Leith Hill from Dorking Station, or Ranmer Common from Box Hill Station (L.B.S.C.R.); those who choose either will certainly not repent taking my advice.

BEHIND SHOOTER'S HILL.

THERE is no town near London so dreary as Woolwich, until you get outside of it; happily, on the high ground, to the south and east, it has three large open spaces, each of which is worthy of a visit. Of Woolwich Common, which is best known, I have already spoken; the other two are Plumstead Common and Bostall Heath, both of them being under the control of the Metropolitan Board of Works. There are many who know

Woolwich itself who have no idea of the beauty of its surroundings. By rail or boat, from any of the piers, or from Cannon Street, Charing Cross, London Bridge, Fenchurch Street, or Liverpool Street, you may reach Woolwich for a return fare of about a shilling, and at Woolwich a tramcar will take you to the further end of Plumstead, or, if you prefer it you may travel direct to Plumstead Station by the S.E.R. Thence by the road which overlooks the Plumstead Marshes, the river, and the low Essex coast beyond, it is but a short distance to Bostall Heath, one of our Metropolitan open spaces which deserve to be better known than at present, commanding as it does on the north an extensive view over the Lower Thames Valley, and on the south an equally commanding prospect over the county of Kent. I would recommend those who do not wish to go far afield, after they have explored the highest points of Bostall Heath, to take the road between the keeper's cottage and the wood, and follow it till they almost reach Wickham Church, a curious old rustic structure, with a red-tile roof and gable windows—and then to take the lane that leads off sharp to the right. Passing by a brickfield, the first lane on the left leads up to Plumstead Common, which is a curious medley of the ancient and modern—of stony wastes and of heathery and fern brake slopes, of high straight levels, and of umbrageous and verdant nooks; of northern smoke and chimneys, and of southern upland meadows and woods. Plumstead Common on its northern side is decidedly inferior to Bostall Heath; but it also has a look southward that is open to the whole face of Nature, and on this side is verdant with fernbrake and purple with heather. Keeping strictly along the road the rambler will at length come upon some wooden steps upon the left, leading up to Shooter's Hill, or he may pursue his road, if tired, straight forward, and subsequently to the right, till again he reaches Woolwich.

For those to whom anything like a circular walk is objectionable, and who require to have nothing to remind them of the dust and drouth of city life from end to end of their ramble, let me recommend Abbey Wood Station as the point of starting (S.E.R., single 1s.). Abbey Wood Station is on the verge of the

dreary Plumstead Marshes, the most prominent feature
in the monotonous landscape being the Southern Outfall
Works at Crossness; but looking to the south there are
pleasant wooded slopes towards which we naturally turn.
According to the guide books the remains of the ancient
abbey are so scanty that they are not worth inquiring
after; the road on the left towards Erith is not par-
ticularly inviting, though if we were to follow it until
we turned up a path through market gardens to Lesness
we should not find it destitute of attractions. We
prefer, however, to keep straight forward up the hill,
with woodlands on either side. If we could only forget
the hard road beneath us, and keep our attention fixed
upon the sylvan charms on either hand, we should have
no reason to complain. Halfway up the hill is a lane
through the woods to the left, which we may follow for
a short distance, but as it is evident that it will lead us
down again towards the marshes we soon retrace our
steps. Returning to the road, we continue the ascent
until we reach a corner of Bostall Heath, where we
may wander at will, though it will be best to keep close
to the northern extremity, up and down the sudden
declivities, till we find it jutting out boldly northward.
The prospect from this point is rather remarkable for its
breadth than for its beauty, extending far across the dull
marshes of the Lower Thames Valley, and somewhat
obscured on the westward by the smoke of the countless
chimneys of Woolwich and the great factories on the
other side of the water. Turning away from this
dubious spectacle, let us pass onward till we reach the
keeper's cottage, and take the road to the left, that
passes between it and the pine wood beyond the heath.
On reaching a signpost we take the road to Wickham
and Welling, and follow it past the quaint little old
church of Wickham till we reach a school. Just beyond
this is a path to the left, which leads us through fields
and orchards into the middle of the village of Welling.
Ever since leaving Bostall Heath we have been traversing
a somewhat flat and uninteresting country, though it
affords us distant views of enticing heights beyond. On
entering Welling we shall find a lane immediately facing
the post-office. A little way down we shall feel inclined

C

to turn back, for it seems, like the American railway, to lead nowhere in particular. However, if we persevere, we shall find that the lane dwindles into a mere footpath, which passes through pleasing meadows; while near us on the left is a park with a shining sheet of water visible between the trees. By and bye the path reaches a perplexing farm road which crosses it at right angles. Here turn to the left for a short distance, and the proper path, striking off again to the right, is soon conspicuous. We will follow this path until it ends in a green lane, where we turn to the left once more, and soon reach a high road. Here we swerve to the right for a few yards and take the first turning on the left, and the first on the left again, when we look out for the first stile on the right. Once across the stile we pursue a somewhat lengthy walk across level meads, until we reach a lane, where we keep straight forward till we reach a main road, and then keep straight forward to the left till we arive at Sidcup Station (S.E.R., single fare 11d.). Although this rural ramble afforded no small pleasure to myself, I must candidly admit that those who require extensive prospects or rich woodland scenery may feel some sense of disappointment; it may be worth while, however, for such people to consider whether it is not their own fastidiousness that is mostly to blame. The most monotonous of fen lands have a beauty of their own if we only take the trouble to discover it, much more the lowlands of the garden county of England. I cannot, however, but admit that it is almost useless to reason with the human eye. Too well I know that I cannot always see with the eyes of others; why should I expect them always to see with mine?

Let me suggest another alternative route, which for its seclusion and beauty it would be difficult to surpass within a dozen miles of the Metropolis. From most of the woods around London the rambler is strictly excluded; rarely, indeed, can we find a path or a lane traversing them. Let those who are tired of the trim London parks, and who thirst for the wild beauty of the woods, accompany me to Pope Street, the next station beyond Eltham on the South-Eastern line (single 10d.). On leaving the station we cross the railway bridge, and find a few yards to the left a lane that re-crosses the railway, which we follow for about a mile through a pretty, but almost level country. When we reach the end of this lane we cross the road, and almost exactly opposite, just a yard or so to the right, we shall find a lane, that soon becomes a mere green track through the woods. For more than two miles we will follow it, under the shadow of the oaks, which have been thickly planted along the greater part of this grassy way. Here and there we catch bright glimpses of distant hills and dales eastward, but on the other side the woodland is continuous to the end. We are but nine miles from London Bridge, yet the solitude is as unbroken as though we were in the remotest corner of Devon or Westmoreland. I have not the pen of John Ruskin, to describe the manifold charms of this delightful piece of sylvan scenery; I would simply urge those who have trusted my guidance before to take an early opportunity of visiting the spot, but not after wet weather. We emerge at the summit of Shooter's Hill, but just at the turn, where the lane becomes a gravel walk, we will pause to admire the prospect beyond the gates leading to a mansion; unfortunately for us who are on the wrong side of the gate, it is only a beautiful vignette. At the top of Shooter's Hill those who are tired may turn to the left, and take one of the roads on the right, leading across Woolwich Common to Woolwich. We, however, will prolong our ramble by turning in the opposite direction. A little way on the right is a private road, into which it is well worth while to deviate, for it commands a wide sweep of country from Bostall Woods to Sidcup. Descending Shooter's Hill we find at the bottom a lane on the left, which we follow till we reach a stile on the left that leads us across upland fields into a lane. Turning to the right we shall soon find another stile leading across another upland meadow, and thus we at length reach Plumstead Common, of which I have already spoken. With the choice of three stations, we naturally prefer the most distant—Woolwich Dockyard—which we reach by keeping along the road skirting the southern side of Plumstead Common, then keeping straight forward till we reach Woolwich Common. Crossing the southern corner of this open space, past the long line of officers' quarters, we turn to the right, and find the station close at hand. The whole distance

described may be rather over eight miles, but at least two
miles may be saved by taking the nearest road to Woolwich Common when at the top of Shooter's Hill. I am
quite aware that I have not done justice to this delightful
walk, and those who follow my guidance will certainly
agree with me.

ELSTREE.

LET us take a peep in Hertfordshire, a county, by the
way, which is not half so well known as it deserves to be.
Every Londoner almost is well acquainted with the
glorious prospect northward of Hampstead Heath; just a
little beyond the range of hills that closes the view is the
hill village of Elstree, a thoroughly quiet, old-fashioned
place, the only buildings of considerable size in it being a
school with a modern red-brick chapel belonging thereto
on the other side of the road. Unfortunately the Station
(Midland) is a mile from the village, yet the surroundings
of Elstree are so pretty that I think it would pay the
Midland to attract a stream of visitors by cheap return
tickets. At present the fare is 1s. single, 2s. return.
Considering the charming character of the country through
which the Midland runs as it approaches the Metropolis, it
seems to me quite possible to attract to it a fair proportion
of the pleasure traffic that now is enjoyed by the Great
Eastern and South-Western Companies, if only favourable
terms were offered. Judging from my own knowledge of
Elstree, and I have visited it several times, it is one of the
most secluded villages within a dozen miles of London.
This alone would be sufficient to recommend it to hard
workers, who seek in their brief half-holidays a maximum
of repose. On a sunny Saturday afternoon I doubt if
among all the thousands that hastened out of London
more than a score or two find their way there. Let those
who, like Cowper, love "the calm retreat, the silent
shade," try it; if they do not all come together they will
be well rewarded.

It might be sufficient recommendation to Elstree to
say that the ever-advancing army of suburban villas has
not yet invaded it, but, besides this, it sits upon a hill
which commands pleasing prospects in almost every direc-

tion, and at its feet lies an extensive sheet of water, which
adds not a little to its attractiveness. The water in
question bears the somewhat repulsive name of reservoir,
but in this case the term is misleading. The Elstree
reservoir has little in common with the formal square
tanks of Battersea or Lea Bridge. If it owes its existence
to art, its surroundings are so natural that its artificial
origin is well concealed. Had I a boy who wanted to
know what a lake was like, I should take him to Elstree.
The local innkeepers claim that when it is not shrunk by
prolonged drought, this sheet of water covers no less than
two hundred acres. Punts may be hired by anglers and
rowing-boats by scullers at very reasonable charges.
Southward, the view from Elstree is bounded by the
contiguous heights of Brockley Hill and Stanmore, but
northward the eye wanders over a wide extent of country,
the ancient Abbey of St. Albans being visible almost due
north. All the approaches to the village are so pleasant
that it matters little whether the rambler reaches it by
way of Edgware, Watford, Barnet, or direct from Elstree
Station. Let us confine ourselves for the present to the
immediate surroundings of the village.

On leaving the Midland Station and reaching the road,
we turn to the left for half a mile, when we shall find a
broad footpath through the upland meadows, which brings
us to the northern end of the village, close to the old
church. This path commands distant views; but if, when
we emerge into the road, we cross it and take the field-
path opposite, we shall be still better rewarded. This
path descends the hill, and leads us into the road to
Aldenham. Here the rambler, if he cares for picturesque
old houses, would do well to turn to the right for half a
mile, when he will find Aldenham House on his right—a
fine specimen of the domestic architecture of two centuries
ago. Otherwise he will at once turn to the left, and he
will soon find a grassy lane on the right hand, which leads
to the Elstree lake. If in no mind for rowing, we can take a
path to the left that skirts the lake for some little distance,
and on reaching a road follow it up the hill to the centre
of the village—or, better yet, when half-way up the hill
we shall find a field-path on the right, our object being to
take a peep over the near hills, which at present shut out

from us the prospect over Middlesex. Some distance
along this path a path branches off to the right, leading to
Stanmore, where we can attain our object, but the nearest
point is Brockley Hill, which we reach by following the
path without turning till it reaches the road at the bottom
of the hill. On reaching the top we find a row of wide-
spreading trees between the roadway and the footwalk.
From the brow of the hill southward the view is somewhat restricted by the foliage, but in the field on the left
the whole of this glorious landscape lies open before us.
Thus far I have written for those who do not care to
wander far from their starting point.

Those who prefer to travel three or four miles further
would do well to take the road to the east from the centre
of the village, leading to Barnet, which affords pleasant
views to the north, and turn down the second lane on the
right, which soon becomes a mere grass track between
ancient hedges. Here the view is even more extensive
than from Brockley Hill. Highwood Hill, Mill Hill,
Hendon, Finchley, Highgate, Hampstead, Harrow, Sudbury, and the long faint line of Surrey Hills beyond lie
open before us. After following this green track for about
a mile we reach the small hamlet of Edgwarebury, where,
turning to the left, by a green-bordered, leafy lane, we
reach Edgware, whence we can return to the City (G.N.R.
or N.L.R.) for a shilling. Cutting out the now superfluous
walk to Brockley Hill and back, the whole distance thus
far described would be no more than six miles.

Though I greatly prefer the above it is well worth
while to indicate one or two alternative routes. First
take the road westward from the centre of the village,
which crosses the southern end of the lake, and follow it
up the long ascent by Caldicote Hall till we reach Little
Bushey Lane on the right. A little way down the slope,
just past some farm buildings on the right, is a stile and a
footpath on the other side of the lane. The prospect at
this point is magnificent, extending far across Hertfordshire,
only more to the west than the Elstree view. After descending into the valley and crossing several meadows, we
at length strike into a lane, when turning to the left we
shall soon find a fresh footpath on the other side of the
lane, leading us up-hill to a corner of Bushey. Here we

turn to the right and keep straight forward for some distance till we find a swing gate on the left, with Watford before us, beyond the intervening fields. The walk is very pretty until we reach the outskirts of the town, and then it becomes somewhat wearisome, the station being situated at the extreme end thereof.

As a second alternative route, we will take the footpath to Stanmore, which is in the road half-way between the village and the lake; only when it forks turn to the right. Or we may take the left-hand one into the road, take a peep over Brockley Hill, and then turn to the right till we reach Stanmore, when we have to the south a similar view to that at Brockley Hill. Let us keep straight forward till we strike a main road at right angles, when, turning to the right, we shall soon reach Stanmore Common and Bushey Heath, an extensive, open tract of common land, at a considerable elevation, and commanding distant views in various directions. It well deserves to be more widely known, though at present its distance from a railway station keeps it very secluded. Like Elstree, it is a place to be kept in mind on Bank Holidays by people who wish to avoid being crowded. Let us still follow the road until we reach the first lane on the left, down which we turn. On the one side of us is the wooded park of Bentley Priory, soon to be the prey of building speculators, on the other is Harrow Weald Common, another secluded heath. Across this common all the way are charming bits of landscape scenery; but we shall find something better still if, on reaching the end of it, we turn down the lane on the right, crossing a corner of the common. Following this we gradually reach higher ground as it winds southward, and soon we find ourselves in front of the view across Middlesex, with the Surrey Hills as a background. The wooded height of Harrow, which is immediately opposite, is nowhere seen to such advantage. Already we have taken the reverse prospect from Hampstead at various points of the ridge, but this view from the southern end of Harrow Weald Common is decidedly the most picturesque of all. Crossing the road, a yard or two to the right is a footpath through a farm, and down a succession of gentle sloping meadows, which at last brings us into a road where we shall find Pinner Station (L.N.W.R., single 1s.)

We have now travelled six or seven miles from Elstree Station; but the rambler who is not yet tired may easily extend his walk by taking a footpath to the right a few yards before reaching the Commercial Travellers' School, which leads up the slope across pleasant meadows, with bright prospects in every direction. This path leads ultimately into Oxhey Lane, when we turn to the left. Thence for two miles we find it a quiet shady lane, with fair prospects of undulating country on either hand, until we reach Watford Heath; rather less than a mile further we reach Bushey Station (L.N.W.R.), which is situated at the southern end of the long main street of Watford. The most picturesque spots in this district are the views from the northern slope of Elstree, from the footpath leading from Bushey Heath Lane towards Watford, and from the southern corner of Harrow Weald; the last for preference may be easily reached by a walk of a mile and a quarter, mostly across the fields, from Pinner Station.

KINGSTON.

Is not this too familiar ground? Surely there are no suburbs more widely known than the riverside villages between Kew and Hampton. Pardon me if I express an opinion that there are plenty of Londoners who might advantageously accept a guide on a tour from Temple Bar to Tower Hill. As for the riverside villages, they are little known to Londoners apart from the river itself. A good walker may take all the places in this district in a single afternoon ramble, though of course he will necessarily leave much unseen, and he need have little but grass all the way along. He has the additional advantage that if he is tired he can break off his journey and take the road home from almost any point.

We commence the combination journey with Teddington, S.W.R. (single 1s.), as our starting point, close to the gates of Bushey Park, with its unrivalled avenue of chestnut trees extending from end to end. Having crossed the park we at once enter the grounds of Hampton Court Palace on the opposite side of the road. Possibly the rambler will take out his map—say that of Smith and Son—and find a road through Hampton Court

Park to the foot of Kingston Bridge. Unfortunately it is no road for him. I cannot but protest against map-makers indicating roads through private parks which are not open to the general public. If there is no thorough-fare for the people who buy the maps, why tantalise them by marking one? As well mark the private grounds of Buckingham Palace Gardens. Hampton Court Park is kept strictly private, except for a few priviledged persons who pay a guinea a year for a key. Some of these days, I suppose, the growing population of Kingston and Hampton Wick will begin to ask why they are jealously excluded from a Royal Park close to their own doors, and will compel the opening of the gates. Bearing a little to the right as we leave the Palace, we shall find a long walk, open to the public, which skirts the river side. At the far end is a door, which is kept locked—a most absurd proceeding, considering that any man can easily jump the low wall that divides us from the path by the river. Even a pair of lovers can easily manage it if they only go back as far as a post that is fixed in the walk below. The only *raison d'etre* for this locked door is that it makes the access to Hampton Court more difficult for the Kingstonians, an attention which they no doubt pro-perly appreciate. Having scaled the wall, there is for three miles a charming walk by the river side, shaded in the afternoon by ancient elms, and with a wide margin of grassy turf. At the end Hampton Wick Station (S.W.R.) is close at hand, but we push forward across Kingston Bridge, and inquire for the nearest gate to Richmond Park, little more than a mile distant. The left hand road will take us to Richmond Hill.

Except at the Richmond Hill and Petersham Gates, this great park is a perfect solitude. I have sometimes sat there on a summer Saturday afternoon, and seen the rabbits playing about as unconcernedly as though all ingress were strictly forbidden. I fact, were I "George Ranger" I would stop the mouths of the Parliamentary Radicals by making a swing gate to each of my great game pre-serves. To Londoners this lonely spot is easily acces-sible on three sides, being little more than a mile from either Richmond, Kingston, or Mortlake Stations. The return fare to this last place from Waterloo is a shilling.

Wandsworth or Battersea residents could easily reach it
on foot, *via* Wimbledon Common and the Robin Hood
Gate. In the spring its wealth of May blossoms is unequalled. People often go to see the chestnuts in bloom
at Bushey Park, but I never heard of anyone visiting
Richmond on account of the fragrant hawthorns. To
my mind, however, the latter sight is even preferable to
the former. Richmond Park, too, extends over high
ground, and, though the central plateau has no special
characteristic, the views from any side of its slopes are
magnificent. As the rambler traverses the road from the
Kingston to the Richmond Gates, especially if he keeps a
little to the left thereof, he will find the prospect across
the Thames Valley most delightful. At the gate we
might part company, but remembering the many who
are not born Cockneys, I will stay to suggest to them that
when they reach the terrace on Richmond Hill they
would do well to descend through the sloping meadow to
the lower road, when a few yards further they may find
their way to the river bank. Passing under Richmond
Bridge, and of course bestowing a glance on the old-
fashioned riverside houses by the way, they will take the
first turning, which leads to the Green, crossing which
obliquely the station is close at hand. The more ardent
pedestrian, however, may follow the river path till he
reaches an entrance to Kew Gardens, after crossing which
he will find the Kew Gardens Station handy for his
return journey to town. There is no need to indicate
the number of miles to be traversed because the pedestrian has the opportunity of leaving off his journey
wherever he pleases at any stage.

For those to whom the various points of this route
are too familiar let me suggest Kingston Station as a
starting point (S.W.R., single fare, 1s.). At Kingston
Bridge we find our way to the river bank through a
narrow street on the right. The river path all the way
gives us pleasant garden views of the Teddington villas,
and for most of the way we can avoid the disagreeable
loose gravel of the towing-path by keeping above it or
below it. A little way beyond Teddington Lock, the
pleasant music of whose weir is suggestive of more
impetuous waters, we shall find a path through a gate

which, striking off through a meadow, soon brings us to
a fine avenue of elms right and left. The high road
forward soon brings us to Ham Street, on entering
which we find on the left an unpromising path between
high walls. This leads us to the entrance gates of Ham
House (Earl Dysart's). All the land about here was
formerly Crown property, but was granted by Charles II.
to Elizabeth Murray, created by him Countess of Dysart,
who married Lauderdale. The very house was fitted and
furnished at the king's expense. Opposite the path by
which we came to this spot is an avenue of trees leading
to Petersham, and here let me suggest to those who find
themselves at Petersham on a school excursion that the
groves of Ham House are quite close at hand, and
are well worthy a visit. Turning our backs upon the
gates, we shall find before us an apparently interminable
avenue of elm trees, about a hundred and fifty on either
side. Many of the old and decayed trees have been re-
placed by young ones, so that the avenue is rather distinguished by its length than by its beauty and symmetry.
In length, however, it is unrivalled by the approaches
of any mansion in the Home Counties. Before we reach
the end we are upon Ham Common, and straight before
us a large white house, hard by which is a gate leading
into Richmond Park. Once through the gate we find
ourselves in a lovely little dell, and on ascending the road
take our choice between the roads to Richmond and
Kingston. We choose the latter. If tired, the rambler
can go out at Kingston Gate, and will find the Norbiton
or Kingston Stations a mile or a mile and a half distant,
handy for his return to town. Let me note here that
many of the S.W. trains to Kingston take a kind of
circular route, and that the way *via* Wimbledon is shorter
and more picturesque than the other.

We who are good walkers will part company with the
tired ramblers that leave the park by the Kingston Gate,
and, instead of passing through the gate, take the road
on the left just inside the park till we reach a short footpath leading through a small gate into the high road.
Exactly opposite us is a road leading through an open gate,
down which we proceed, despite its private appearance.
Woodlands are on the one side, flower-beds on the other;

the broad-spreading oaks close by the foot-way affording us grateful shade. Occasionally we have distant glimpses of the sylvan valley of the Thames. When at length we strike into the high road, we turn to the right. The first footpath to the left leads us through broad, level meadows, though after passing the first field we must be careful to make a little deviation to the right in order to find the path. After crossing a railroad bridge another footpath to the right through the meadows will bring us to Norbiton, and so once again to Kingston.

Close to Kingston Bridge is a capital coffee tavern for tired wayfarers. In some of our crowded London thoroughfares the coffee tavern movement has thrust itself where the keen competition of private enterprise had made it almost unnecessary, but in the outer suburbs it is really a great boon to the public. A dozen years ago the hot and thirsty pedestrian had no choice at all. He had to drink beer or almost equally thirst-provoking ginger-beer. Now-a-days it is different. Not only at populous places like Woolwich, Croydon, Kingston, and Woodford, but in such rural villages as Carshalton and Winchmore Hill, he may avoid the public-house altogether. Even in an old-fashioned town like Barnet I came across a capacious inn converted into a commodious and well-conducted temperance restaurant. This is not a matter that concerns teetotallers alone. There are thousands who like a glass of ale at the half-way house, but most decidedly prefer a cup of tea and yet more solid refreshments at the end.

MILL HILL.

WESTWARD from the great high road between Finchley and Barnet run three hill ridges, traversed by roads. The most northerly, running from Barnet towards Elstree, is not an attractive highway, though at a distance the slope looks pretty enough. The most southerly, Mill Hill, joins the central one of Totteridge. Among these verdant hills and dales more than one pleasant afternoon may be spent. Let us first take one or two short journeys that will fatigue no one, and give the rambler plenty of time to rest wherever he pleases.

We take Totteridge Station as our starting point (G.N.R., single 9d.), and take the road along the top of the hill westward toward Edgware. Apart from the commanding views which it affords it is in itself a charming road, well wooded, green bordered, and at intervals adorned with ponds in which are water-lilies and other aquatic flowers. Though we might turn off by a path at Totteridge Church, we will follow this delightful road till we reach on the left, between two ponds, three field gates. It is the furthest of the three gates which leads us into a footpath across the meadows. Losing sight, as we descend, of the distant heights of Muswell Hill, Highgate, and Hampstead, we find the scene midway between the two ridges quite as pleasing, if more contracted. Ascending the Mill Hill slope, we at last strike into the road, when we turn sharp off to the right up the hill between arching trees on either hand. As soon as the trees are passed, there is a footpath to the left across high ground, which gives an extensive prospect eastward, and on leaving this, and taking the road opposite us, the woody heights of Hendon lie straight before us to the south. A short walk brings us to Mill Hill Station, G.N.R. (single 8d.), about four miles from our starting point, the greater part upon green turf.

For those who prefer a walk a mile or two longer I would recommend a still more picturesque route. Starting from Totteridge Station and along the road to Edgware, we pass the path by the three gates, and take the next on the same side of the way, crossing the same valley. On reaching the main road at Mill Hill we turn to the right for some distance, at intervals pausing to admire the noble prospect both northward and southward, especially the latter. The broad valley of Central Middlesex is now full in view, the wooded height of Harrow rising like an island in the sea of verdure. Following the main road, past a red-brick convent, and avoiding the narrow lane on the left, we shall find straight before us, when the road turns as it descends the hill, a swing gate, which once more brings us into the fields. The path is hardly marked as we descend, but across the field we see a stile, having passed which we find the track easy, up a gentle ascent from which

the view is exquisite. Descending on the other side, we
emerge where three lanes meet, but almost opposite us, a
little to the right, is a stile, through which we pass into
the next valley, with High Barnet full in sight. Thence-
forward we pursue our way, and return to town from
High Barnet Station, G.N.R. (single 9d.). It is worthy
of mention that at Totteridge once resided Lady Rachel
Russell, and at Mill Hill William Wilberforce.

As an alternative route, let us approach Mill Hill
from the south. In some respects this way is superior,
and the Midland Railway charges but 1s. for a return
ticket from Moorgate Street. At Hendon Station we
take the road up the hill, which, by the way, commands
an extensive prospect westward. Opposite some old
almshouses we find a turning to the left, which soon
brings us to Hendon Church. The view northward from
the churchyard comes upon us as a pleasant surprise,
commanding as it does the wooded slopes of the range of
hills that runs along the northern boundary of Middlesex.
Passing out of the churchyard at the eastern end we find
a footpath before us, which soon strikes across open
meadows, and affords us at different points bright
glimpses of the surrounding country. This path extends
almost to Mill Hill. When at length we turn into the
lane we climb the hill and find the outlook far more
extensive than from Hendon Churchyard. On reaching the
main road we turn to the left; for some distance we have
picturesque panoramic views on either hand. When at
length the road swerves a little to the right, we shall see
straight before us a lane with posts across it, with a
sharp descent. It soon turns to the left, and a few yards
further on the right is a field-gate, on the other side of
which is a footpath. By no means miss this deviation, for
though Mill Hill is beautiful from every vantage-ground,
this path is the best of all. On a clear calm summer
evening, looking southward, beyond the intervening
heights, the long unbroken outline of the Surrey Hills is
plainly visible, and here and there in the gaps westward
are the dim blue lines of far distant heights, on whose
identity the rambler may speculate as he pleases, the
dark, wooded ridge of Harrow and Sudbury rising pro-
minently in the middle distance. At the end of this path

is another gate leading into a road; but, instead of
climbing it, let the rambler take a path to the left down
the slope, which all the way is grateful both to his feet
and his eyes. When at last he reaches a road, he will
turn to the right towards a railway station, and the sign-
posts will direct him back again to Hendon. When once
again at Hendon Church he need not keep to the road.
The lane that descends the hill in front of the church has
a stile a few yards down on the left, across which there
is a pleasant path through the meadows, leading into a
lane. Follow the lane to the right, and after passing a
small stream look out for the first stile to the left, which,
crossing meadows again, brings us into the Edgware
Road, where, turning towards London, we soon find ourselves at the road on the left which leads us to Hendon
Station. The lady must be a poor pedestrian who finds
this delightful route beyond her powers, and it has the
double advantage that, while for every yard of the distance it affords picturesque views of the surrounding
country, the greater part of the way is through open
fields.

I have kept that which I consider the best route till
the last. It has the greatest variety of views, is almost
all footpath, and is progressive, not circular. What
further recommendations can it require ? Let the rambler
take the road up the hill from Hendon Station (Mid.)
above described, to Hendon Churchyard. After passing
straight through the churchyard, instead of taking the
path before him let him take the path to the left. He
will soon find himself in the open fields overlooking the
valley of Central Middlesex, with a wide prospect extending from Hanwell southward to Elstree and Pinner
northward, the midway heights of Harrow being a
prominent feature in the scene all the way, till he reaches
a shady lane, where he will turn to the right up the hill.
Where the lane strikes into a road the rambler will see,
almost exactly opposite him, a stile and footpath leading
over a rising ground. Along this footpath charming
views open out in all directions. On a summer evening
the long bold outline of the Surrey Hills stand distinctly
in view in the extreme distance. Possibly the dim line
that fills in the valley between Harrow and Pinner is

still more remote. South-east the prospect is more limited, being bounded by Finchley and the Alexandra Palace. When once more we strike into a road we turn to the right and take the furthermost of the two forks. We look out for the first stile on the left, and, following the path, we shall soon find ourselves in the grassy valley between Mill Hill and Totteridge, with Highwood Hill at the head of the valley to the left.

Let us keep along the path till we at last ascend the further slope and reach Totteridge Church. In the churchyard itself we shall find a fair prospect northwards, and a little beyond it a wide open space with a road leading to the right. Totteridge Station is close at hand, but the green-bordered road is so attractive that we follow it, and we shall find ourselves well rewarded for the trouble. At the end of the road is a stile leading by pleasant meadows to Torrington Park Station, G.N.R. (fare $8\frac{1}{2}$d.). The path all the way commands very pleasant views of the wooded country around Mill Hill and Totteridge. It was possible to have reached Torrington Park by a little more direct footway, but I am confident that no one who has followed my deviation will complain at having had to walk an extra mile. The whole distance of this route is not much more than six miles, and for four-fifths of the way the rambler is under no necessity to keep to hard roads. The fields are almost all under grass, an advantage which those who are familiar with ploughed fields in early spring, and stubble fields in late autumn, will duly appreciate. London excursionists seeking for fresh fields and pastures new, could hardly do better than explore the delightful scenery around Mill Hill.

SUBURBAN SURREY COMMONS.

As I wrote on Hampstead chiefly for the benefit of South Londoners, so I speak of the suburban commons of Surrey chiefly to induce North Londoners to visit them. Probably not a few South Londoners may find some hints as to beauties to them hitherto unknown. The corresponding prospect to the northward view from Hampstead Heath is the southward view from the terraces at the Crystal Palace. Glimpses of it may be caught from various standpoints,

but from the Palace alone is this wide prospect to be seen
in all its wide extended beauty. He who has gazed on
that knows the fairest landscape that South London can
boast. The ridge from South Norwood to Forest Hill
has been so entirely appropriated by upper middle-class
villas that it is disappointing to the pedestrian unless he
takes delight in their trim lawns and bright flower gardens.
I confess that to me they are always too suggestive of
painful contrasts with the stifling courts of St. Giles's,
Drury Lane, and East London; apart from this they are
pleasant enough to the eye, though they shut one out from
the noble prospect beyond. Westward of this ridge the
the country, happily, is more open.

A good walker might easily take the four commons in
this quarter in a single afternoon—viz., Clapham, Wandsworth, Tooting, and Streatham, the two latter being by
far the most attractive. The whole circuit I am about to
take would be nearly twelve miles, but the distance may
be contracted at any stage. The trams bring the rambler
to the Clapham Common starting point; he may cut off
two miles by booking from Victoria to Wandsworth Common (L.B.S.C.R.), or another mile by booking to Balham
on the same line, or he may go to Streatham Common
direct either from Victoria or London Bridge, or by
'bus from the City. The fares are but a few pence to
any point. On reaching Clapham Common keep the
Balham Road in sight, which skirts the left-hand side of
the common; but on passing the second pond keep straight
forward a little further from the road till, at the extreme
end of the common, Nightingale Lane is reached. On
emerging from Nightingale Lane, we cross a corner of
Wandsworth Common, and take the first turning to the
left after passing over the railway bridge. I note that in
this road the villa-builders have left many of the ancient
trees unmolested—a course which should enhance the
value of the property, and which on that account I recommend to the imitation of the great firm of Vandal and
Company elsewhere. This road takes us into the highway to Mitcham, when, immediately opposite, we find a
lane which soon brings us to Tooting Common. Considering how great was the struggle for this open space, I fear
it has never yet been fully appreciated. It is true that it is

as level as a fen, but for sylvan beauty there is no suburban common that surpasses it.   If a lazier pedestrian than ourselves joins us from Balham Station, after finding his nearest way to the common, he will find his path lies through a noble grove of elms ; we who are traversing the right-hand side of the common find our pathway shaded all along by an equally ancient row of trees.   At the end a short lane leads us by Streatham Church on the one side, and a quaint red-brick mansion flanked by dark cedars on the other, to the high road leading to Streatham Common.

Streatham Common is shaped like an hour-glass; the lower lobe a grassy upland, the higher thickly covered with furze.   From the upper part the southward and westward views are magnificent.   The high road skirting the common on the left, and leading to the Crystal Palace, is at various points as attractive as any suburban road can be; but, with our natural preference for footpaths, we break away from the road at the pond mid-way over the common, and pursue the second path on the left, which at the end of the common leads us into the open fields. Here the view is less obstructed than from the common itself.   At the end of the footpath is a lane on the right leading us back by a green track into Streatham ; but if we are not tired we shall do well to turn the other way till we reach a high road, and then turn to the right past the Conquering Hero, and take the first or the second lane to the right—the latter for preference.   This lane soon becomes a mere footpath across grassy meadows, with the villa-crowned ridge of Norwood behind us ; and at length we emerge into a lane, only passable in fine weather, where, if we turn to the left, we shall by and bye reach Thornton Heath, whence we can return by train to Victoria. As no fresh beauties are to be discovered in this direction, we will turn to the right, and follow the lane till it brings us back into Streatham.   On the southern side of London there is no spot within seven or eight miles of St. Paul's where the London rambler can so easily forget his proximity to the great City.   There are other paths besides those that I have mentioned, but these will suffice.   At present, at any rate, the charms of rural solitude are within the reach of the poorest denizen of Lambeth.

East of the Crystal Palace there is but one common of considerable size, and the encroachments of modern builders are more disagreeably intrusive; yet the district is well worth a visit to those who are unacquainted with it, inasmuch as it possesses at least one elevated spot which is unique in its beauty. Rye Lane, Peckham, may be reached by either the L.C.D.R. or the L.B.S.C.R. A short walk brings us to Peckham Rye, a pleasant open field, much used by cricketers. The road skirting the Rye on the right will take us to Honor Oak direct; but we will take that on the left, which, if followed, brings us into a footpath at the corner of Nunhead Cemetery. Here, turning to the right, we follow the pathway to Brockley, which gives us pleasant glimpses of the surrounding country all the way. On reaching the road we turn to the right, and follow it to the first footpath, which leads us, slanting, across the fields, then over the railway bridge into Honor Oak Park. Up the slope is a new church, behind which we climb to higher ground, and find that around us is an almost circular panorama. In this respect its completeness is unique; let those who doubt put it to proof. Only at one point—to the south-west—is there any break in the distant prospect. Starting from this point, the eye rests first upon the south-western suburbs with faint outlines of hills beyond, then there is the long wooded ridge of Champion and Denmark Hills with more distant spires peeping above the foliage. Then there is a valley with Peckham in the foreground, and beyond it the wide extent of Central London, the towers of Westminster, and the dome of St. Paul's standing out clear above the smoke. A little further eastward the hill behind the Rye and Nunhead Cemetery somewhat hide the view, but a strip of south-east London is clearly visible beyond. In the next break we look right across New Cross, Deptford, Greenwich, and the Isle of Dogs. Then the eye rests upon the high ground of Blackheath, and in the next break we look across Lee and Lewisham. Further on is the wooded slope of Shooter's Hill, and the distant prospect takes in the country round Eltham, Chislehurst, Plaistow, Bromley, Bickley, Keston, Hayes, Knockholt, and the hills of Addington; while in mid-distance are Catford Bridge, Dartmouth Park, Forest Hill, and half-a-dozen other pleasant suburban villages. The hill on which we are standing is private property, but it is open to all visitors; I thank its owner for affording me the opportunity of seeing that which is now the most extended view of the Metropolis and its southern suburbs. It may be worthy of notice, as we have reached the spot in my accustomed round about way, that it is but a few minutes' walk from Honor Oak Station (L.D.C.R.); on leaving the station turn up the road away from London, and take the first road on the left.

Honor Oak Station is close at hand, but a good pedestrian will naturally desire to continue his ramble. Unfortunately I can show him nothing to equal the hill of Honor Oak. On coming down from the hill he will follow the road till it strikes into the main road, where he will turn to the right till he reaches the station. Here he will find a pleasant road between the station and the cemetery, which brings him into Lordship Lane, when, turning to the right till he reaches the "Grove Tavern," he will find opposite a grove of young trees slanting to the left. At intervals there are very pretty views, more especially when he takes the footpath that crosses the line. This brings him to the road that runs along the top of Sydenham Hill, where he has little to interest him except the trim villa gardens, though occasionally right and left are bright glimpses of the country beyond. On arriving at the "Dulwich Wood Tavern" he may descend by a fenced pathway through the enclosed Wood of Dulwich, opposite Sydenham Hill Station, or he may continue his walk a little further to the Crystal Palace Parade, which affords a view of Dulwich, Gipsy Hill, Tulse Hill, Herne Hill, and other outer southern suburbs. Retracing his steps a little till he comes back to the eastern end of the Palace, he will find a road that leads down to Sydenham Hill Station. Here let me interject a hint to Crystal Palace visitors on popular firework nights. If you wish to avoid the rush to the station, book by the main line L.D.C.R. to Sydenham Hill, and walk up the road to and down on the return from the Palace. It costs no more and saves the disagreeable crowding. If the rambler wishes to walk further on reaching Sydenham Hill Station, let him follow the road, till he almost reaches the "Greyhound Tavern."

Then take the lane on the left, which leads him into a footpath that leads across the level meadows. Crossing a new road a little to the left, he will find another path leading under the railway arches, and thence to the road which, to the left, leads to Herne Hill Station (L.D.C.R.). The whole distance from Peckham Rye Station to Herne Hill by the route indicated is about eight miles, and may be cut short at almost every stage. For those who do not care to walk far, let me repeat that the chief points of interest in this article are the fields behind the upper part of Streatham Common, and the circular panorama from the hill at Honor Oak Park.

THE KENT AND SURREY BORDER.

FOR a final ramble let me invite my readers to the border land between Kent and Surrey, between Caterham and Westerham, a district known to very few, far out of the beaten tracks of travel, where the ubiquitous bicycle seldom penetrates—soon, however, to lose its seclusion, though I would fain hope but little of its beauty. Let our starting point be Warlingham Station (S.E.R., single 1s. 3d.), in the Caterham Valley. Those who are satisfied with a walk of three miles each way may take a return ticket; wiser and hardier walkers will do otherwise. Let us turn along the road southwards toward Caterham, till we reach a lane on either hand, and just beyond these, on the left, take a road through an open gate (Marden Park), with a park lodge at the side thereof. For some distance we are upon level ground, with pleasant near views of the surrounding hills; but when we pass under the lofty arches of the line now in course of construction a fresh prospect opens before us eastward. Marden Park is, I think, the most picturesque portion of the Caterham country, and the higher we climb the greater is our gratification. Once through the arches we take the left-hand road till we reach the corner of a wood that stretches far up the hill. There is a footpath up the hill-side on the right, just before the wood is reached, which we follow, now and then pausing to admire the view of the Caterham valley and the villa-crowned hills beyond. After a while the path merges into a wide, new-made road, which con-

tinues to ascend the hill until when the summit is reached
the wide sweep of country, from the towers of Sydenham
to the woods of Reigate Hill, lies open before us. Just
beyond is a tiny cluster of cottages which form the hamlet
of Woldingham, passing by which, along a narrow lane
which takes us to yet higher ground, we see to the right a
rustic church, which rivals in its diminutive size the far-
famed smallest church in the Isle of Wight. All the way
we have kept in sight of the distant hills, but there is a
point a little way beyond the church where we must pause
awhile to admire the exquisite beauty of the scene. Turning to the right we see at but a short distance a kind of
hollow basin, whose depth is concealed by its thick woods,
a little sea of rich verdure, above which is a broad bright
belt of greensward, beyond it line upon line of dark
wooded heights, and yet in the extreme distance faint
hazy glimpses of the remoter hills. Immediately before
us westward is the sombre shoulder of Reigate Hill, then
the distant view is broken by the intervening height
of White Hill, easily distinguishable by its mansion and
isolated tower; then a little further southwards stands out
the long promontory of Leith Hill, its watch-tower a mere
speck in the distance; and due southward—but for that
let us wait till we find a little further a narrow lane on
the left, which ascends for some distance along the top of
the ridge. If we proceed along this lane for two or three
minutes we shall find a point where we have the most
complete view southward and northward.

Mr. Ruskin, when writing of mosses, says—"No words
that I know of will say what these mosses are—none are
delicate enough, none perfect enough, none rich enough."
If the greatest of our prose poets confesses the insufficiency
of his wealth of words to depict " the rounded bosses of
furred and beaming green," how can I venture to describe
one of the noblest landscapes of Southern England—this
solitary sanctuary of the hills, overlooking broad valley
lands, which have been but made more beautiful by the
homely industry of a hundred generations! A little below
the point at which we are standing was the great pilgrim
way to the shrine of A'Beckett at Canterbury; but I am
dreaming of the earlier time, when the great forest of the
Weald stretched from the foot of this ridge to the South

Downs overlooking the Channel. There are still large dark patches of forest country, especially on the broken slopes of the Wealden ridge; but in the lower lands, copse and cornfield, meadow and hop-garden, homestead and hamlet, are delightfully intermingled as far as the eye can reach. At the foot of the steep on which we stand we can descry village after village nestling peacefully amid the dark foliage, and beyond, where the eye fails to distinguish these, an immense stretch of undulating country, that seems to extend to an almost illimitable distance, with here and there remote heights so faint and far that, like Long-fellow's *Preciosa*, we are ready to admit that we see them rather with the heart than with the eyes. In the middle distance, to the right, is the soft sylvan slope that stretches from Godstone towards Redhill, looking across which we can take in the great plain of Mid-Sussex. The corre-sponding ridge to the left, which includes Toys Hill and Ide Hill, is still more thickly wooded, and gradually rises to an altitude that shuts out the view over Tunbridge and Mid-Kent. Now let us turn and look northward and westward across the hill country. The dells are so narrow and the downs so broad that the immediate prospect seems somewhat tame; but beyond the eye takes in a wide range of country, extending in a grand semi-circle from Gatton Park to Shooter's Hill, with faint grey lines here and there, far beyond the points that we can recognise. The loveli-ness of this spot is only equalled by its transcendant beauty. So fair and gracious a landscape as this, once seen, becomes one of those precious treasures of memory which neither moth nor rust doth corrupt, and into which no thief can break through and steal. As Jean Ingelow reminds us, there is a deep true sense, in which " memory is possession ;" in the heart of the great city, I thank God to-day that I am the richer for this bright vision of the world that lies beyond the hard, stony ways of daily life.

And now it is time that we should part company with the Warlingham return-ticket holder, who will, of course, return by the way whence he came; our destination is Westerham, which lies some six, or seven miles further on. For half the distance the lane proceeds along the top of the ridge, sometimes through ancient woodlands, that shut us in from the outside world, sometimes with

occasional glimpses between the bosky slopes of the fair
meads below, here and there with a wide extended view
of the rich southern landscape. After a while, having
passed two lanes that lead up to the little village of
Tatsfield, we find that the road turns downward toward
the valley, and at length we shall see Westerham at some
distance on the right. There is a footpath here which
cuts off a good corner of the road, but turns into it again
after crossing the corner of one of the many hop-gardens
in this neighbourhood, which, in early autumn, are in
the full perfection of their beauty. We follow the road,
past the gasworks, till we reach the outskirts of the little
town, and then we shall find a small stream flowing along
the left-hand side. Just after passing a little brick
bridge we shall find a green-painted wooden bridge leading into a path across the fields to Westerham Station
(S.E.R.), from whence we can return to town, though I
may remark in passing that this valley by way of
Brasted to Sevenoaks is well worthy of exploration.

Taking Caterham, Sevenoaks, and St. Mary Cray as
the three angles of a triangle, I may remark that the
whole of the country between is well worthy of a visit.
There is hardly a village included therein which has not
a beauty of its own. I have only space now to indicate
one route in particular—that between Shoreham and
Knockholt. Shoreham (L.C.D.R., single 1s. 9d.) is
situated in the beautiful valley between Swanley Junction and Sevenoaks, which lies before us on the right as
soon as we pass the tunnel between Swanley and Eyns-
ford. On leaving the train at Shoreham we turn to the
right through the village, where, by the way, before
reaching the church, is a pleasant footpath to the left
leading to Otford, a village down whose streets run clear
bright streams, and just across whose green is a portion
of the ruined palace of the Archbishops of Canterbury,
now converted into a blacksmith's shop. We follow the
village street of Shoreham till we reach the new Wesleyan
Chapel, opposite which we shall find a footpath leading
up the hill-side, where we will pause to admire the scene
around us. We are now close upon a wood. Unlike
many suburban landowners, Mr. Mildmay, of the great
house of Baring and Co., does not shut out his woods

from wayfarers, for which I heartily thank him. We take the first track to the left through a pretty avenue of trees, and at length arrive upon open ground, where another charming little valley meets our gaze. Just after passing some farm buildings we turn to the left once more through the woods, where, by the way, nuts are plentiful, and immediately emerge from there at the "Polhill Arms." Immediately opposite this hostelrie is a lane which slants off between the main roads, and some little distance down we find to the left another bye-way through the woods again. After a while we shall reach a point where there are two or three tracks, where we keep straight forward, avoiding those to the left. Some distance further an oak tree marks the point where we should turn to the left. A few yards further, and we reach a green track, where we turn to the right and keep straight forward through the woods till we reach Knock-holt. On reaching the road we turn to the right, and inquire for Halstead Station, keeping straight forward for some distance. Just after passing a cluster of trees on the left we shall find a stile on the same side of the road which leads through a pleasant undulating park. On reaching a lane we turn to the left for a few yards, and find a path across the fields, which we steadily pursue until we find divergent paths, where we take the left-hand one, which leads us to Halstead Station, from whence we can return to town (S.E.R., 1s. 2½d.). Those who love woodlands and undulating parks and meadows will find this a most charming route, the walking distance between the two stations being only between six or seven miles.

Printed by COOK, AUSTIN & Co., 3, 4 and 5, Swan Buildings, Moorgate Street, London, E.C.

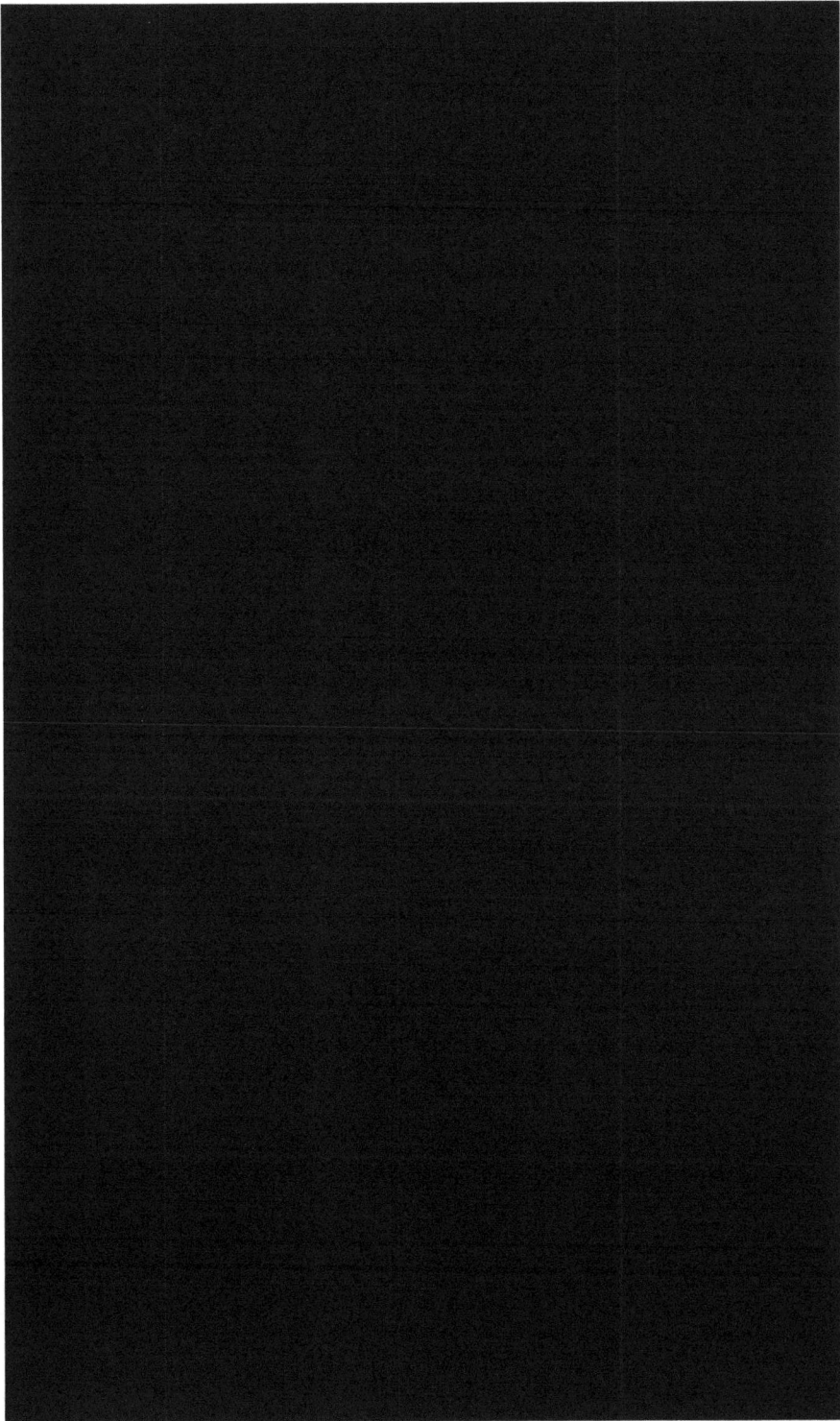

Lightning Source UK Ltd.
Milton Keynes UK
UKHW031843300819
348851UK00004B/152/P